THE TRIGRA

THE TRIGRAMS
OF HAN

Inner Structures of the I Ching

STEVE MOORE

THE AQUARIAN PRESS

First published 1989

© STEVE MOORE 1989

British Library Cataloguing in Publication Data

Moore, Steve
The trigrams of Han.
1. Confucianism. I Ching
I. Title
299'.51282

ISBN 0-85030-808-9

The Aquarian Press is part of the Thorsons Publishing Group, Wellingborough, Northamptonshire, NN8 2RQ, England

Printed in Great Britain by Mackays of Chatham, Kent

1 3 5 7 9 10 8 6 4 2

Contents

For Liz,
With Love.

Preface

Since the 1960s, interest in the Chinese *I Ching*, the Book of Changes, has risen to unprecedented levels in Europe and America. It has gained an enormous popular reputation as a work of divination, a reputation no doubt enhanced by the interest shown in it by the psychologist C. G. Jung. As a result, translations, popularizations and works of interpretation have flooded onto the market in recent years. It may therefore seem superfluous to add yet another volume to an already expansive literature.

However, this is not another work on divination, and is intended for the reader whose interest in the *I Ching* extends beyond its predictive use. Its subject matter is at once both smaller and larger than the Book of Changes. Smaller, in that it deals primarily with the eight trigrams and their various arrangements, correspondences and uses, rather than with the hexagrams and texts of the book itself. Larger, in that it examines the concepts related to the trigrams in a much broader context: as part of an all-encompassing cosmological and cosmographical system which developed, for the most part, from quite separate roots. It is a system which sought to explain the nature of the world and its processes in terms of the Five Elements, yang and yin, the directions, numbers, the trigrams and so forth, correlated together like interlocking rings. This system survives in the commentaries to the *I Ching*, as well as in a number of other independent texts from the same period. As we shall see, though, there is no evidence of it in the original text of the *I Ching* itself. It is a product of much later correlative thought, which can be shown to have reached its greatest state of elaboration during the Han dynasty (202 BC–AD 220).

Unfortunately, the reputation of the *I Ching* as a book of 'ancient

wisdom' is such that it has become commonplace to simply accept
everything in it, both text and commentary, at face value. This is
as true of some of the book's finest translators as it is of its
popularizers, and more often than not the traditions attached to
it are simply repeated unquestioningly, while totally disregarding
the sinological work of the last 50 years. This is not surprising.
Much of this sinological research is both technical and inaccessible
to the general reader, and he may find its conclusions unpalatable.
It is to be hoped that the reader's interest is sufficiently strong to
allow him to withstand a number of surprises as we delve deeper
into the subject. We shall have to deal rather firmly with the
traditional material, examining both its chronology and its
authorship. The results of this examination will show that the
chronology must be revised to give later dates than those commonly
accepted for both the commentaries and the text of the *I Ching* itself;
and in the process the connection with the book of such famous
names as Fu Hsi, King Wên and Confucius will necessarily be
exposed as the fictions they really are.

Nonetheless, this is not simply a work of destruction. In clearing
away the dead wood of tradition, the text of the *I Ching* itself is
left largely untouched, and for those whose interest in the book
lies primarily in its value as a divination manual, nothing at all
is lost. However, with the dead wood removed, it is possible to
shed a much clearer light on the commentatory material
surrounding the *I Ching*, and specifically on that part of it which
deals with the eight trigrams and their part in the correlative system
of the Han dynasty. That the material with which we have to deal
is the work of anonymous authors of a later date than previously
thought does nothing to destroy the intrinsic interest or value of
the system itself. Indeed, dating the material to the Han period
opens the way for new interpretations and speculations, and allows
us to offer possible solutions to a number of problems that have
remained unsolved for many years.

This is a book of researches, compiled over a number of years.
As such, it owes an enormous debt to previous scholars in the field,
and the reader will find this debt acknowledged in the references
and bibliography. My gratitude is no less deeply felt where, on the
odd occasion, I have cause to disagree with the opinions of these
authors. It is in the nature of such research that problems arise
where solutions may differ, or where no definite answer appears

to be possible. Such problems may still be examined, however, and where necessary I have allowed myself the freedom to offer speculations, no matter how tentative, where positive answers are not possible. Hopefully such speculative material will be immediately apparent to the reader, and will be seen to be within the context of the material.

My thanks are also due to a number of friends for various assistances; locating valued reference material, commenting on and correcting my manuscript, and so forth. Most of all, I have to thank them for their whole-hearted encouragement over a lengthy period of time. In no order of preference, they are: Liz Barnden, Mike Crowley, David Fideler and Alan Moore. I have profited enormously from their support, though ultimately I must take responsibility for all that appears here.

Strange as it may seem, there is one more debt of gratitude to record: to Chu-ko Liang (AD 181–234), of whom I will have more to say in Chapter 9. It was with him that my researches began; without him, none of what follows would have been written.

A Note on Transliteration

In common with most other books on the *I Ching* (and especially with the translation of Richard Wilhelm and Cary F. Baynes, to which the majority of references will be made), Chinese words are here romanized according to the Wade-Giles system of transliteration, rather than the more modern New Chinese Phonetics. Perhaps it could be argued that we should move with the times, but it seems to me that any advantage this might have would be far out-weighed by the disadvantage of rendering such commonplaces as *I Ching*, *Ch'ien* or *Chên* as '*Yi Jing*', '*Qian*', and '*Zhen*'.

Part One
Opening The Way

1
Basic Groundwork

It is to be hoped that the reader will have at least some basic familiarity with the *I Ching*, of which the recommended edition would have to be that of Wilhelm and Baynes[1]. Although this is now some 60 years old and in need of a certain amount of revision, it is still the most complete modern edition, and is the one to which most reference will be made in the pages that follow.

Blofeld's translation[2], although more recent, lacks many of the commentaries that play an important part in the material assembled here. Legge's edition[3], although containing the commentaries, is awkward and outdated. Perhaps the most interesting recent edition is that of Whincup[4], which takes into account many of the textual emendations suggested by recent scholarship. It does not, however, translate any of the commentaries.

Whincup's interpretation of the text is frequently idiosyncratic and made largely from a divinatory point of view. As an example, Wilhelm gives the trigram Sun the meaning of The Gentle, with additional meanings of wind and wood. Whincup renders this as 'Kneel in Submission', which may well be the original meaning of the word, but he ignores the additional meanings. From a philosophical and cosmological viewpoint, however, wind and wood are the major attributes of Sun. The use of the *I Ching* as a divination manual has, perhaps, been over-emphasized. By the Han dynasty at the latest it was seen as a major philosophical work on the nature of change and its symbolic system had been fully integrated into a correlative cosmology. In such a context, a narrow definition of Sun as 'Kneel in Submission' is quite irrelevant.

Most of the other editions of the *I Ching* currently on the market are of little value beyond their use as the most basic fortune-telling devices. In some cases, where the text has been 'rewritten for modern readers' or reinterpreted from a particular narrow viewpoint, the results can be downright misleading. It is true that the *I Ching* developed in a particular historical and geographical context, and reflects the social conditions and concerns of its time. Nevertheless, it is a symbolic work, and its symbols transcend its context. When this is properly understood, its judgements have universal application. To remove it entirely from its context and rewrite its symbols narrows the field of application and destroys the philosophical system it contains. At worst, it can result in a distortion of the meaning which is quite inappropriate to the original. Besides, the basic assumption of any such revision must be that the perpetrator 'knows better' than the original authors which, at best, is arrogant; at worst, disastrous.

For the benefit of those who might not be familiar with the commentaries on the *I Ching*, and for those to whom a summary of Chinese cosmology might be useful as a quick reference, this chapter provides a succinct look at some of the basic philosophical concepts and systems. Most of these concepts originated shortly before the Han dynasty, although their integration together is largely a product of that period. I shall have more to say about their historical context in the chapters that follow.

Yang and Yin

One of the basic principles which became common ground to all schools of Chinese philosophy was that of dualism, in that the universe was seen as being shaped by two opposing but complimentary principles, known as yang and yin. Originally, the word 'yang' seems to have meant the southern, sunny side of a hill, while 'yin' meant the northern, shaded side. However, by about the fourth century BC the meanings of yang and yin had expanded to take in a number of other concepts[5]. Some of their major attributes are as follows:

Yang: positive, masculine, light, the sun, day, high ground, activity, dryness, fire, the South, heaven.

Yin: negative, feminine, dark, the moon, night, low ground, passivity, moistness, water, the North, earth.

Such lists could be extended further, but these examples should be sufficient. There are a number of things to point out here. Firstly, we are not talking about two types of physical matter; there is neither pure 'yang stuff' nor 'yin stuff' in the universe. Instead, we are dealing with a relational concept: the 'yang-ness' of one thing by comparison with the 'yin-ness' of another. A couple of examples may make this clearer.

If we compare the sun and moon, then undoubtedly the sun is yang, the moon yin. If we compare the moon and stars, though, the moon, being more bright, is yang while the stars are yin. Similarly, on a human level, a wife is yin, her husband yang. However, if the wife has a female servant their relationship has to be defined separately. Rather than a male-female relationship, we now have one of mistress-servant; the wife is yang, the servant yin. [6]

Nor should we make a simplistic correlation that yang is good and yin bad. In purely philosophical terms, yang and yin have complete equality, being no better or worse than one another than are the positive and negative poles of a magnet. In Chinese popular culture, however, there is a tendency to give preference to yang over yin. Again, this will be best demonstrated by examples, which will also give some suggestion as to how such a situation came to be.

Traditional Chinese society was masculine-dominated with a patriarchal lineage system. The need for male offspring to carry on the family line thus caused a major over-emphasis on the yang principle in a very fundamental area of human existence. This emphasis appeared not only in a desire for male children, but also in the social emblems attached to marriage and childbirth. Once again, the concept is relational: a Chinese bride was dressed in the yang colour red as a potential mother of boys, rather than in the yin colour blue that one might expect to fit her role of wife to her husband.

As with life, so with death. A human being was conceived as having two types of soul, the yang *hun* and the yin *p'o*. Assuming all went well, the *hun* soul ascended to heaven after death and became a *shên*, a spirit. The *p'o* soul, however, remained earthbound after death. If, for instance, the ancestral sacrifices were neglected, it was likely to become a *kuei*, a malignant demon or revenant, wreaking vengeance on its still-living descendants. All devilry was thus seen to be yin and, by association, the yin became something to be avoided [7].

Returning to the concepts of yang and yin as abstract principles, it should be pointed out that their relationship is not static. The universe as a whole seeks balance between the two, but there may be local imbalances leading to the preponderance of one principle over the other for a period of time. Such an imbalance is not permanent, however, and the very nature of change itself is seen as an alternation between the two. First yang succeeds yin, then yin succeeds yang[8]. Indeed, if one principle becomes overly exalted at the expense of the other, it turns into its opposite. Thus when the yang reaches excess, it turns into yin, and vice-versa. Each principle is thus said to contain within itself the 'seed' of the other, as is well illustrated by the often seen circular diagram of yang and yin, shown in Figure one. Here yang is represented as white, yin as black. The 'comma-shape' of the yang contains a black dot (the 'seed' of the yin) at its broadest point, and vice-versa.

Figure 1

In the hexagrams of the *I Ching* the yang is represented by an unbroken line, —, known as a light, firm or undivided line; the yin by a broken line, - -, known as a dark, yielding or divided line. The divination method of the *I Ching*, be it using coins or yarrow-stalks, provides four possible numbers connected with each line of a hexagram: six, seven, eight and nine. Seven represents a stable, unchanging yang line, while nine represents a changing yang line; one which will, in the secondary hexagram, turn into its opposite, a yin line. Similarly, eight represents a stable yin line, six a changing one.

The Eight Trigrams

When the yang and yin lines mentioned above are arranged in groups of three, eight possible different arrangements result. These are known as the *Pa Kua*, the Eight Trigrams.

In each trigram, the 'first' line is the lowest, the third or 'last' being uppermost. The 'movement' within each trigram, from one to three, thus goes upward. Similarly, and rather more importantly, this concept of 'movement' is also applied to the hexagrams, where the motion is from the bottom, first line, toward the top, sixth line.

The lowest line of the trigram is connected with Earth, the second with Man, the third with Heaven. This linked trinity of Heaven, Earth and Man is another basic conception in early Chinese philosophy. Heaven was thought of as round, and the rotating sky was constantly in motion. The major luminaries, sun, moon and stars, were also placed in the heavens. Heaven was thus seen as yang. Earth, which was thought to be square, did not move and was not luminous; it was therefore yin. Man was seen as the intermediary between the two. Having the greatest capacity for direct action, be it for good or evil, Man was thought to be at least equally as important as the other two members of the trinity, if not the most important.

Each of the trigrams has a number of symbolic attributes, and a summary of the most important ones is given in the table that follows. The major source for these attributes is the appendix to the *I Ching* known as the *Shuo Kua Chuan*, the Commentary on the Trigrams[9], from whence comes most of the following information, only the exceptions being referenced.

≡ *Ch'ien*. Being composed entirely of unbroken lines, Ch'ien represents yang in its purest form. Its meanings include the Creative, Heaven, the strong, the active, the father. Its Element (see next section) is Metal.

☷ *K'un*. Composed entirely of broken lines, K'un represents yin in its purest form. Meanings include the Receptive, Earth, the weak, the passive, the mother. Its Element is Earth.

☳ *Chên*. The Arousing, Thunder. Movement and, less commonly, earthquake ('movement within the earth')[10]. It represents the eldest son (the lone yang line is said to 'control' the other two yin lines, and so to indicate the sex of the trigram; as the yang line appears in the first place, it is designated the first or eldest son). Its Element is Wood.

☴ *Sun*. The Gentle. Wood. Wind. Penetration. The eldest daughter. Its Element is Wood.

☵ *K'an*. The Abysmal (the depths). Water. Danger. The moon. The middle son. Its Element is Water.

☲ *Li*. The Clinging. Fire. Lightning. The sun. The middle daughter. Its Element is Fire.

☶ *Kên*. Keeping Still. Mountain. The youngest son. Its Element is Earth.

☱ *Tui*. The Joyous. The Lake. Mist or clouds[11]. The youngest daughter. Its Element is Metal.

The trigrams are frequently arranged in circular sequences, two of which are well known, a third being rather more obscure. The discussion of these arrangements will form the substance of Part Two.

The Five Elements

In the West, in ancient and medieval times, the universe was interpreted in terms of Four Elements (Earth, Fire, Air and Water). A similar theory developed in the East, but in China the Elements numbered five: Wood, Fire, Earth, Metal and Water. The Chinese character for Metal, *chin*, can also be translated as 'gold'. In this context, however, Metal is the usually accepted meaning.

There is some evidence to suggest that in ancient times these Elements were thought of as the real physical substances that they were named after [12]. By Han times, however, this narrow concept had been expanded, and the Elements were also thought of as cosmic forces or principles, the interaction of which was seen as a major agent of change. As a result there have been a number of attempts in recent years to find an alternative to 'Five Elements' as a translation of the original Chinese phrase *Wu hsing*: Five Forces, Five Agents, and so on. The most popular of these has been 'Five Phases', but this does not seem to be entirely satisfactory either. True, Five Elements may seem to over-emphasize the meaning of physical substances without including the concept that they are agents of change. On the other hand, Five Phases seems to throw the baby out with the bath water, implying that we are dealing only with stages in a cycle of transformation quite divorced from the real, physical world. And for all their interest in constructing neat cycles of transformation, the primary object of the Han cosmologists was still the interpretation of the real world. Perhaps a translation along the lines of 'Active Principles' might better encompass both aspects of the *Wu hsing*.

All this aside, I have decided to continue using the term Five Elements for the very simple reason that this is how *Wu hsing* is translated in most of the literature on the *I Ching*. There seems no point in adding further confusion to an already complex subject.

The Five Elements can be arranged in a number of cyclical orders. Mathematically, there are 36 possible combinations, but only two have any importance to the material with which we are dealing, those of Generation and Destruction[13]. The cycle most commonly encountered is that of Generation, in which each Element gives rise (or gives birth) to the one following it, thus:

Wood generates Fire
Fire generates Earth
Earth generates Metal
Metal generates Water
Water generates Wood

The cycle then starts again from the beginning, and continues in unending circles. These relationships naturally require some further explanation, and the traditions that have come down to us vary from the obvious to the extremely forced.

Wood generates Fire: this is explained by the fact that wood provides the fuel for fire. Fire generates Earth: the ash left by a fire is interpreted as earth. Earth generates Metal: metal ore is found in the earth. Metal generates Water: here we have two explanations, first, that when metal melts it becomes liquid; second, that water condenses on bronze mirrors that are exposed to the air overnight. Water generates Wood: plants (wood) absorb water in order to grow.

The second major arrangement is that of the Destruction Cycle, also known as the Cycle of Conquest, as follows:

> Wood conquers Earth
> Earth conquers Water
> Water conquers Fire
> Fire conquers Metal
> Metal conquers Wood

Again, the explanations occasionally seem rather dubious. Wood conquers Earth: wooden spades are used to dig up the earth. Earth conquers Water: earth absorbs water. Water conquers Fire: by extinguishing it. Fire conquers Metal: by melting it. Metal conquers Wood: metal axes and saws are used to cut wood. It is sometimes said that the cycles must be seen as starting with Wood, or again that they must start with Water; but this seems to depend on an over-literal reliance on particular ancient texts, with complete disregard for other equally ancient texts which start the cycles with different Elements. For our purposes we can treat them as ever-revolving circles and, as that sage wit Charles Fort once remarked: 'One measures a circle beginning anywhere' [14].

The Directions

To the usual four compass points, the Chinese added a fifth 'direction', the Centre. This may seem surprising at first, but it had considerable value in the Han correlative system to be examined in Chapter 3. Attempts were made to group things in fives (directions, Elements, colours, flavours, planets, parts of the body, and so forth, the list extending almost indefinitely), and then to correlate them together.

South is always placed at the top of Chinese maps and diagrams related to the cardinal points. If not taken as another example of 'the Chinese doing things backwards', this is usually explained by simply saying that the Chinese considered South as the most important direction. To a certain extent this is doubtless true. China being in the Northern hemisphere, the southern half of the sky is that through which the sun travels, and is thus the direction of the yang.

However, there may well be more to it than that. In ancient times, the possession of maps was an imperial prerogative, and this was taken extremely seriously. So seriously, in fact, that one of the charges brought against Liu An, the Prince of Huai-nan (under whose direction the classic Taoist-eclectic book, *Huai-nan Tzu*, was written), was that he and his magician-associates had made use of maps[15]. This hardly seems a serious accusation at first sight (though I shall have more to say on the subject in Chapter 3); but Liu An was none the less executed for treason in 122 BC.

If the Emperor alone was allowed to use maps, then obviously they would have been designed for his convenience. The Emperor's throne was always positioned to face toward the South, the direction of the yang. Therefore, in order for him to make the correct orientation with the cardinal points, it would be natural for any map spread before him to have the East on his left hand, the West on his right; with South furthest away from him, at the top of the map. [16]

Some Western authors, presumably working on the assumption that they will have remarkably few Emperors among their readership, tend to reverse Chinese cosmic diagrams so that North is at the top. As we shall see, this can have some extremely regrettable consequences, so the original Chinese usage will be continued here. The 'compass' will thus appear as in Figure 2.

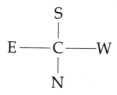

Figure 2

Some of the important directional correlations were as follows:

The South's Element is Fire, its colour red. Its symbolic animal is the Red Bird.

The West's Element is Metal, its colour white. Its symbolic animal is the White Tiger.

The North's Element is Water, its colour black. Its symbolic animal is variously given as a tortoise, a tortoise entwined with a snake, or as a god known as the Dark (or Mysterious) Warrior.

The East's Element is Wood, its colour is *ch'ing*, which can be translated as either blue or green. Perhaps some such colour as turquoise was intended, but in this context it is often translated as 'azure'. The West's symbolic animal is the Azure Dragon.

The Centre's Element is Earth, its colour yellow. In Han times it appears to have had no symbolic animal, instead being represented iconographically by a mound[17]. However, in later times it seems to have been thought necessary to give it an animal to match the other directions; this is given variously as an ox or a yellow dragon.

The Ten Celestial Stems and Twelve Terrestrial Branches

From ancient times the Chinese calendar has been based on a cycle of 60. This sexagenary cycle is known to date back to the Shang dynasty (eighteenth to twelfth centuries BC; see the table of Chinese dynasties at the end of this chapter), when it was used for designating the days of the year. Its use for the numbering of the years themselves seems to date only from the Hsin interregnum between the two halves of the Han dynasty[18].

This cycle was evolved by combining a set of symbols known as the Ten Celestial Stems (perhaps the names of the days in an ancient 10-day week) with another set known as the Twelve Terrestrial Branches (perhaps derived from the number of months in a year)[19]. The Ten Celestial Stems were correlated with the Elements and the directions, as follows:

1.	Chia	Wood	East
2.	I	Wood	East
3.	Ping	Fire	South
4.	Ting	Fire	South
5.	Wu	Earth	Centre
6.	Chi	Earth	Centre
7.	Kêng	Metal	West
8.	Hsin	Metal	West
9.	Jên	Water	North
10.	Kuei	Water	North

It may be noted here that the Elements are arranged in the order of the Generation Cycle. The Twelve Terrestrial Branches play a lesser part in the system that relates to the trigrams, but they are given here for the sake of completeness. They correspond with the animals of the Chinese zodiac, and with the 12 double-hours of the day.

1.	Tzŭ	Rat	11 p.m. — 1 a.m.
2.	Chou	Ox	1 — 3 a.m.
3.	Yin	Tiger	3 — 5 a.m.
4.	Mao	Hare	5 — 7 a.m.
5.	Ch'ên	Dragon	7 — 9 a.m.
6.	Ssŭ	Snake	9 — 11 a.m.
7.	Wu	Horse	11 a.m. — 1 p.m.
8.	Wei	Sheep	1 — 3 p.m.
9.	Shên	Monkey	3 — 5 p.m.
10.	Yu	Cock	5 — 7 p.m.
11.	Hsü	Dog	7 — 9 p.m.
12.	Hai	Boar	9 — 11 p.m.

The sexagenary cycle was formed by combining these two cycles. A particular day or year would be designated by two symbols, one Stem and one Branch, and the two series ran in parallel. The first day would thus be Chia-Tzŭ, the second I-Chou, and so on. The eleventh day would be Chia-Hsü, the twelfth I-Hai, the thirteenth Ping-Tzŭ. Only after 60 combinations (60 being the lowest common multiple of 10 and 12) would the two series line up again at Chia-Tzŭ, and the cycle would recommence.

Numbers

All odd numbers are considered to be yang, or Heavenly. All even numbers are yin, or Earthly. Particularly important are five, the number of the centre; nine, the highest of the single yang numbers; and 10, which represents a complete cycle.

The Trigrams of Han

Simplified Table of Chinese Dynasties

	BC		AD
HSIA dynasty (Legendary?)*	2205–1766		
SHANG (or YIN) dynasty*	1766–1122		
CHOU dynasty*	1122–221		
Spring and Autumn Period	722–480		
Warring States Period	480–221		
CH'IN dynasty	221–206		
HAN dynasty	202	—	220
Earlier (Western) Han	202	—	9
HSIN dynasty (interregnum)			9–23
Later (Eastern) Han			23–220
THREE KINGDOMS Period (Shu, Wei, Wu)			220–265
CHIN dynasty			265–420
NORTHERN AND SOUTHERN dynasties			420–581
SUI dynasty			581–618
T'ANG dynasty			618–906
FIVE DYNASTIES Period			906–960
SUNG dynasty			960–1279
Northern Sung			960–1126
Southern Sung			1126–1279
YÜAN (Mongol) dynasty			1279–1368
MING dynasty			1368–1644
CH'ING dynasty			1644–1911

* Dynasties marked with an asterisk are represented here by their traditional dates. These are a matter of some dispute.

2
The Historical Context

A detailed examination of the eight trigrams cannot be made in isolation. They are embedded in a much larger cosmological system which includes the Five Elements, yang and yin, the Celestial Stems, and so on. This cosmological system itself has been drawn together from a number of components, and it is important to have some idea of how these components are related historically, both to each other and to the trigrams. As an example, there would be no point in interpreting an arrangement of trigrams in terms of the Five Elements if the trigram arrangement could be shown to have come into existence several hundred years before the theory of the Five Elements was first formulated. We need to know not only when the cosmological system was put together, but also to have a realistic idea of when the trigrams first appeared. To deal with the trigrams, it is necessary to investigate the extremely complex history of the *I Ching* and its commentaries. The age of this material lies at the heart of the problem, so it will be as well to start with the *I Ching* itself.

There is, of course, a traditional history attached to the *I Ching*, attributing its origin to the sages of antiquity. This history dates back at least to the Early Han period, and is mentioned by Ssu-ma Ch'ien, China's greatest historian (145–86 BC)[1]. Two thousand years of repetition, both in Chinese and Western languages, has meant that it has often been accepted uncritically. Briefly, it runs as follows:

The eight trigrams were invented or discovered by the legendary Emperor and culture-hero Fu Hsi, whose traditional dates vary wildly from the thirty-ninth to the thirtieth centuries BC. Fu Hsi was also said to be responsible for the circular arrangement of the trigrams known as 'The World of Thought', an arrangement which sometimes bears his name (see Chapter 5). In some versions of the tradition he is also said to have doubled the trigrams to make the hexagrams.

More often this doubling of the trigrams to make the hexagrams is attributed to King Wên, the progenitor of the Chou dynasty. All the sources seem agreed that King Wên actually wrote the texts attached to the hexagrams as a whole ('The Judgements'). He is said to have written these while imprisoned by the tyrannical last emperor of the Shang dynasty which, according to the traditional dating, was overthrown by the Chou in 1122 BC. King Wên is also said to be responsible for the 'World of the Senses' arrangement of the trigrams (see Chapter 4).

The judgements to the individual lines of each hexagram are said to have been written by the Duke of Chou, a son of King Wên. The commentaries collectively known as the 'Ten Wings', which form all the rest of the *I Ching* apart from the above-mentioned judgements, are said to have been written by Confucius; or if not by that philosopher himself, by his most immediate disciples[2].

For all the many virtues of Wilhelm's translation of the *I Ching*, it has to be said that he seems to have accepted and transmitted this traditional history quite uncritically, paying little attention to the dating of any part of the text or commentaries. As the most complete version, however, Wilhelm's has become the 'standard translation' on which Western interest centres. More popular works on the subject have transmitted the traditional history in their turn, citing Wilhelm as their authority. This has resulted in the *I Ching* gathering a reputation as an 'ancient wisdom' book of nigh-on prehistoric origin. It is thus much-beloved of occultists, theosophists and followers of the so-called 'perennial philosophy', who seem to see in it a system of thought which reached a complete and perfect state in a time of great antiquity.

This repetition of the traditional history is an interesting phenomenon in itself as, quite simply, there isn't a word of truth in it. Even more interesting is that it is still being repeated despite the fact that it was first questioned several centuries ago in China, and totally destroyed by modern sinology in the last 60 years or so.

Unfortunately, the writing of history is not an exact science, and the contents of histories and traditions are frequently subject to manipulation, whether it be for political, philosophical or other reasons. Examples can easily be found in the West: the unfounded notion of the Roman people's descent from the Trojan, Aeneas; the fathering of Alexander the Great by Zeus, and so on. We shall return to the subject of *why* this fraudulent history was constructed a little further on. First, we must try to get a true picture of the history of the *I Ching*.

Regrettably, English translations of the *I Ching* have a tendency to confuse matters by integrating a certain amount of the commentatory material with the original core text of the book. The first task, then, is to distinguish between the two. The core of the text consists of nothing more than the Judgements to each of the hexagrams (attributed to King Wên) and the Judgements on the individual lines (attributed to the Duke of Chou). This material is sometimes known as the *Chou I*, the 'Changes of the Chou dynasty'. Everything else (The Image, The Sequence, The Commentary on the Decision, and so on) is later commentary. As even the traditional history admits that the *Chou I* is older than the commentaries, let us turn our attention toward that first.

It might be assumed that the text and the hexagrams were contemporaneous creations, totally dependent upon one another; but this is not necessarily the case. Taking them in isolation, we shall deal first with the actual text itself, rather than the linear figures of the hexagrams. This is obviously not the work of a single hand, or even of one person following closely the work of another (the Duke of Chou following King Wên). Several separate elements can be distinguished in the text.

The oldest part of the text is the individual line judgements. The judgements to the hexagrams as a whole are thought to be later additions[3]. These provide summaries to each group of line-texts and define the 'area of interest' covered by them. This, of course, reverses the order of the traditional history. However, as the line-texts themselves can be shown to be a heterogeneous collation from at least three sources, with different elements appearing in the same hexagram, it could hardly be otherwise. If the summaries had existed first, the line-texts would undoubtedly have shown greater uniformity.

The three main sources for the line-texts can be defined as follows:

1. Peasant omens that we would classify today as 'popular superstition'. These are similar to the English 'Red sky at night, shepherd's delight', and some are actually in rhyming verse. An

example may be found in hexagram 31, Influence, which seems to refer to a perception of tinglings in various parts of the body, and the meanings attributed to them[4].

2. References to historical figures and events in the late Shang or early Chou dynasties[5].

3. Simple mantic phrases such as 'Good fortune', 'Perseverance', 'Success', and so on, deriving from practical divination. These phrases are probably later than the peasant omens and historical references, possibly being added when the divinatory applications of these references were no longer immediately apparent[6].

Undoubtedly some of this material, particularly the peasant omens, derives from oral tradition which could easily have existed separately from the hexagrams. This may well be very ancient, but naturally it would be impossible to date its origin. Instead, we are forced to look for the time when this diverse material was first brought together and written down to form the text we possess today.

The problem is made more difficult by the fact that, in places, the text is obviously corrupt. Classical Chinese is always written with extreme brevity, and this is especially true of the *I Ching*. The meaning of a text can be totally changed if a single character is written wrongly, or if the meaning of an ancient character has changed or been forgotten. Later commentators and translators therefore have to rely on previous commentatory apparatus to derive the true meaning of the text, and that commentatory apparatus is not always correct. It may be well to point out that both Legge and Wilhelm made their translations from editions of the *I Ching* prepared in the Sung dynasty (AD 960–1279), using the Sung commentatory apparatus[7].

As an example, let us look at hexagram 35, Progress. In the judgement to the hexagram as a whole, the phrase *k'ang hou* appears. Wilhelm translates this as 'the powerful prince', taking *k'ang* as 'powerful'. However, it actually means 'The Lord of K'ang', a particular place, and was a title of the Prince of Wei[8]. This prince was a relative of the house of Chou.

A number of similar historical references have now been recognized, and Whincup's translation of the *I Ching* is the first to take these revisions into account[9]. These references have led some scholars to place the origin of the text near the beginning of the Chou dynasty (about the eleventh century BC) on the grounds that these historical events must have been relatively fresh in the writers' minds. This is not a convincing argument. In a Western context, such a theory would lead us to move Homer back from his usually accepted date of the eighth century BC to the tenth or eleventh, because he 'must' have lived shortly after the Trojan War in order to write *The Iliad*. Besides, persons connected with the founding of states and dynasties (such as Romulus, Alexander the Great and William the Conqueror) tend to stay in the mind for centuries; especially in a civilization so well aware of its own history as China. All that can be really said on these lines is that the text must be later than the events to which it refers.

Probably the most detailed philological study of the *I Ching* in a Western language is that of the Russian scholar Shchutskii. He came to the conclusion that the written version of the text could not have come into being before the eighth century BC, because its language differs from the archaic forms that are found in divinatory texts inscribed on oracle bones up until this time[10].

However, Shchutskii also concluded that the text cannot be later than the seventh century BC. This conclusion rests mainly on the fact that quotations from the *I Ching* appear in the *Tso Chuan* (Master Tso's Commentary on the Spring and Autumn Annals). This is a very knotty problem.

The *Tso Chuan* is a chronicle of historical events that occurred between 722 and 468 BC. The earliest quotation from the *I Ching* appears in connection with events dating from the year 685 BC. Shchutskii therefore concluded that the *I Ching* must have been in existence before this date[11]. But are these references genuine? Both Shchutskii and Hellmut Wilhelm think they are[12].

Obviously, the *Tso Chuan* cannot have been written before 468 BC, the last year that it chronicles, and Shchutskii is prepared to accept that it may be as late as 300 BC. The references it contains to the *I Ching* are very detailed, including not only the hexagrams but the individual lines derived during the divination as well. That such detailed minutiae should have survived for more than three centuries is surprising, though not impossible. Anachronism is not impossible either, and is, indeed, quite common in early Chinese texts. Perhaps the best that might be said is that the *I Ching* was known to the author of the *Tso Chuan*, some time during the fifth or fourth centuries BC.

Unfortunately, this is by no means the end of the problem, for the authenticity and dating of the *Tso Chuan* itself has been impugned, and there is a school of thought which would have it that the text was retouched and expanded about 250 BC, at which point it is possible that the quotations from the *I Ching* were inserted[13].

Similar accusations of interpolation or textual corruption are aimed at a number of other early references to the *I Ching*. In short, there is no mention of the *I Ching* in a text that is acceptably reliable to everyone before the late third century BC[14], which has led to speculation that it did not exist before that date. Such ideas have been current since Chêng Ch'iao first expounded them in the twelfth century AD.[15] This view is perhaps a little extreme, and certainly represents the latest end of the spectrum in dating.

However, even if we did settle for a date sometime between the eighth and third centuries BC for the writing of the text, this would still have to be regarded as only one fixed point in its continuing evolution, and a fairly arbitrary one at that. The production of a written text would, to a certain extent, 'crystallize' a number of older traditions and preserve some ancient material. But it is by no means certain that the *I Ching* referred to in the acceptably reliable sources of the third century BC is exactly the same as the text we possess today. Continuing revisions are possible and, indeed, seem highly probable.

Shih-chuan Chen has pointed out that a number of quotations from the *I Ching* given in ancient sources do not appear in the edition we have today[16]. These sources include *The History of the Han Dynasty*, *The Travels of Emperor Mu* and, interestingly, the *Tso Chuan*. Whether one regards the quotations from the *Tso Chuan* as early or late, in some places they are quite clearly not quoting from the *I Ching* that we possess. For example, hexagram 18, Work on What Has Been Spoiled, is quoted as having a judgement of 'A thousand chariots retreated thrice. As the result of the three retreats a male fox is captured'. Again, for hexagram 24, Return, we are given 'The Southern kingdom is routed; shoot at its king and hit one of his eyes'[17]. There are no judgements remotely resembling these in the current edition.

We do now possess an early manuscript copy of the *I Ching*, written on silk. This was excavated in 1973 from the No. 3 Han tomb at Ma-wang-tui, near Changsha in Hunan Province[18]. The manuscript can be dated fairly precisely to the first half of the second

century BC. It is written in the standardized characters introduced
by the Ch'in dynasty (221–206 BC), and the actual burial took place
in 168 BC. The hexagram and line judgements are substantially
the same as those in the modern edition, although the names of
the hexagrams themselves frequently differ. These variant names
carry different meanings, although it is quite possible that in ancient
times they had a similar pronunciation to the Chinese characters
used today. Three examples (out of many) will show the differences.
Ch'ien, The Creative, is rendered as *chien*, the bolt of a lock; *K'un*,
The Receptive, as *ch'uan*, streams, or to flow; *P'i*, Standstill, as *fu*,
a wife or woman[19]. Curiously, in his translation Whincup is
extremely inconsistent in his use, or not, of these Ma-wang-tui
variants[20]. The silk manuscript also gives the hexagrams in a totally
different order to the sequence in current editions of the *I Ching*.
They are arranged in groups of eight. Each of the hexagrams in
a particular group has the same trigram in the upper position, and
they are then ordered within the group according to the familial
aspects of the lower trigrams[21]. Full details of this sequence will
be found in Appendix One.

   This mention of varying sequences of hexagrams brings us to
another item of traditional history. According to this, there were
two 'Books of Change' prior to the *Chou I*. First is the *Lien Shan*,
said to be the Book of Changes of the Hsia dynasty, and to have
begun with the hexagram *Kên*, Keeping Still. Second is the *Kuei
Ts'ang*, said to be the Book of Changes of the Shang dynasty, and
to have begun with the hexagram *K'un*, The Receptive[22].

   Needless to say, if these works actually existed at such an early
date and used the hexagrams, this would have disastrous
consequences for the traditional history that states that King Wên
doubled the trigrams to make the hexagrams. The *Lien Shan* and
Kuei Ts'ang have not survived. One or two quotations purporting
to come from the *Kuei Ts'ang* have been preserved, but these are
of a purely mythological nature[23]. Mention is made of both works
in various texts, but these are mostly of a comparatively late date:
the *Chou Li* (Han dynasty), the *Hsin Lun* (Han) and the *Shan Hai
Ching* (parts of which are perhaps as old as the fourth century
BC, although the whole was edited and expanded in the fourth
century AD). The *Lien Shan* is said to have contained 80,000 words,
the *Kuei Ts'ang* 4,300. This has led Chinese scholars to ask the
obvious question: if the *Lien Shan* belongs to the Hsia dynasty

and the *Kuei Ts'ang* to the Shang, why is the later text so much
shorter than the former? Surely one would expect an expansion
of the text, rather than a contraction. The possibility has been
mooted that all mention of the two texts is a result of forgery in
the Han dynasty[24].

If the *Chou I* itself can be shown to date no earlier than the middle
of the Chou dynasty, rather than the beginning, it seems highly
unlikely that the *Lien Shan* and the *Kuei Ts'ang* date from the Hsia
and the Shang. Apart from anything else, there is no evidence
of the written Chinese language existing before the Shang dynasty.
Henri Maspero was of the opinion that the *Kuei Ts'ang* dated from
the fourth century BC, and that it was said to be the Shang
recension of the *I Ching* because it originated in the land of Sung,
which was occupied by descendants of that dynasty[25]. This may
be a reasonable proposition. If the *Lien Shan* and *Kuei Ts'ang* existed
at all, it seems most likely that they represent different schools of
interpretation of what was basically the same book, rather than
earlier versions. When the *Chou I* became the 'established text', it
may be supposed that these variant schools then faded into
obscurity.

As far as the *Chou I* itself is concerned, we are obviously dealing
with a text drawn from diverse origins, of uncertain and possibly
varying dates, which remained in a fluid state until relatively recent
times. If the text is drawn from various separate sources, some of
them perhaps oral, it is quite possible that the text (or at least parts
of it) originally existed quite independently of the hexagrams. It
now becomes necessary to ask what exactly are the linear figures
of the hexagrams themselves?

One thing that is generally accepted is that the hexagrams did
not derive from 'King Wên doubling the trigrams'. There is no
mention of the trigrams in the *Chou I*, only in later commentaries,
and it seems certain that the six-line hexagrams had priority, and
that the trigrams were derived from them[26].

It is possible to see this process at work in the text as we now
have it. The title of hexagram 36, *Ming I*, is usually translated as
Darkening of the Light. Waley shows that a 'Ming I' is actually
an unidentified type of bird[27]. This makes much more sense in
the context of the individual lines, with their reference to wings
and flight. However, by the time the text reached its final recension,
and the commentaries were written, the original meaning of 'Ming

I' had obviously been forgotten. The hexagram was thus reinterpreted in terms of the trigrams that compose it, Li, light, under K'un, earth, to give a meaning of Darkening of the Light. At the same time, *Ming I* was split into two words, *Ming*, 'bright' and a rare meaning of *I*, 'injury'.

Where then do the hexagrams come from, if not from the trigrams? It has been suggested that the linear figures derive from an ancient form of arithmetic, which used the number five as a base, rather than the denary system we use today[28]. This is similar to Roman numerals, where six is VI (5 + 1), seven is VII (5 + 2), and so forth. This ancient arithmetic was performed with counting rods, used in a similar fashion to the sliding balls of an abacus. Obviously, the manipulation of counting rods for arithmetic, and of yarrow-stalks for divination, represent two very similar processes. Needham has also shown that one of the Chinese characters used for 'calculation' is very closely related to the word for 'divination'[29]. The actual numerals used in relation to this counting rod arithmetic are also extremely suggestive, and are shown in Figure 3.

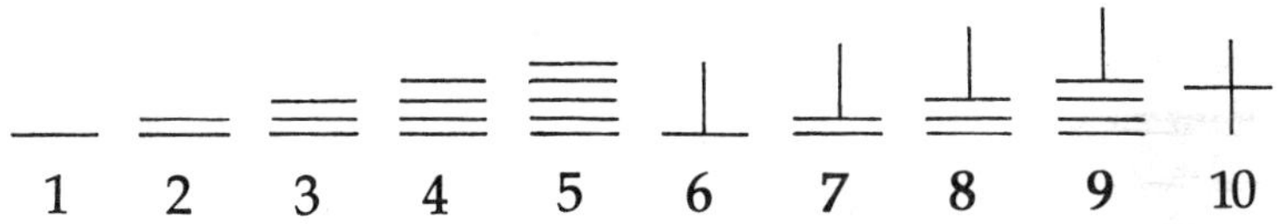

1	2	3	4	5	6	7	8	9	10

Figure 3

Here the numbers from one to five are represented by a simple piling up of horizontal lines; for higher numbers, the five is represented by a vertical line, and then the horizontal lines are added beneath to make up the rest of the number. It has been suggested that the broken lines of a hexagram represent the figure one, the unbroken lines five[30]. It would seem more logical to me, however, if the suggestion were to be reversed; that the unbroken lines represent one, the broken lines five.

Needham suggests that the hexagrams would thus have been a degeneration of an ancient form of arithmetic. However, the hexagram figures obviously cannot be numbers in themselves, representing the numbers one to 64. It would, for instance, be impossible to make numbers less than six with a hexagram formation. The famous circular arrangement of the hexagrams, in

which correspondences have been found to Leibniz's binary
mathematical notation for the numbers zero to 63, is a much later
development, invented by Shao Yung (AD 1011–1077)[31]. We have,
rather, to look for two *similar* processes. In one, the mathematician
manipulated counting rods to produce linear patterns, representing
numbers. In the other, the diviner manipulated yarrow stalks to
produce linear patterns which were used as keys to identify various
oracle texts.

If these 'key' linear patterns do indeed have their origin in an
arithmetic based on the number five, and if the maximum number
of lines in any counting rod numeral was five, it might be
conjectured that, originally, the figures could possibly have
contained only five lines, rather than six. In this case, we would
expect to find that the oracle texts attached to them would also
contain only five lines. There is, in fact, some evidence to suggest
that this was the case.

Hexagram 31, *Hsien*, Influence, refers to perceptions in various
parts of the body. Five of the line judgements contain the word
hsien and also refer to parts of the body; the fourth line does
neither[32]. Hexagram 52, *Kên*, Keeping Still, also refers to parts of
the body. The word *kên* appears in all six lines, but one line (the
sixth) does not refer to a part of the body[33]. Furthermore, on
consulting the Chinese text, we find that in hexagram 36, Darkening
of the Light, the words *Ming I* appear in only five of the line
judgements[34]. In hexagram 5, Waiting, the word *hsü* (whether one
translates it as 'waiting' or, as Waley gives it[35], 'some form of insect
or worm') only appears in five of the lines[36]. In total, there are 14
of these 'five line' hexagrams, where the key word (the name of
the hexagram) appears in five of the six line-places: numbers 4,
5, 15, 18, 23, 27, 31, 33, 36, 41, 52 (see above), 56, 58, and 59.

Combinations of broken and unbroken lines in five-line figures
would only give 32 possible variants, of course. This would
probably have been insufficient to handle the number of oracle
texts in use, especially if the collection of such texts was an ongoing
process. We can therefore suppose that a sixth line was added to
the figures to bring the number up to 64. At this point it would
be necessary to interpolate a sixth line into the five-line texts already
existing. Some of these interpolations are easily distinguishable,
as shown above; others would seem to have been more skilfully
done.

If this theory is correct, there would be two distinct stages in the correlation of the text and the linear figures; the first stage with figures of five lines, the second with figures of six lines. This may suggest an early short edition existing before the long version that we have today. Such an edition would use five-line figures. Obviously, these five-line figures could not be constructed by doubling two three-line trigrams. The invention of the trigrams would thus have to date from a period contemporary with, or later than, the construction of the six-line figures.

A summary history of the *Chou I*, then, would probably go something like this. First to originate would be the omen-material contained in the text. This was of diverse origin: peasant omens, mantic formulae and historical recollections. Some of this material may be far more ancient than the written text, handed down by oral tradition. This material was then collected together and 'keyed in' to the linear figures of yarrow-stalk divination. It seems quite likely that in the first stage there were only 32 texts, and the linear figures consisted of five lines only. With further collection of oracle texts it then became necessary to expand the system, producing a new edition of 64 texts, keyed to 64 figures. Part of this process of integration would have been the addition of the phrases 'Nine at the beginning', 'Six in the second place', and so on, to the original oracle texts. At some point during the collation of this material, it can be assumed that the judgements to the hexagrams as a whole were added, summarizing the material contained in the line judgements. The text then remained in a fairly fluid state, with variant readings and differing orders of the hexagrams, until it was finally 'fixed' in the state that we have it today. All the analytic material contained in the commentaries (trigrams, line correspondences, appropriateness of place, 'holding together', and so on) is later than the text itself. Assuming this scheme of development to be correct, the construction of such a complete logical system of interpretation to explain and justify a conflated text of diverse origins, combined with a symbolic 'indexing' system of differing origin again, is truly a remarkable achievement. Rather more remarkable, perhaps, than the traditional explanation which starts with the trigrams, doubles them to make the hexagrams, and then attributes the judgements according to the supposed internal logic of the structure.

If all this has laid the ghosts of Fu Hsi and King Wên to rest, there still remain some outstanding questions about the *Chou I*. When did the text finally become 'fixed' in the form that we have it today? Why was the traditional history invented in the first place? And what is the relationship of Confucius with the book? These questions can be dealt with together.

The most likely date for the fixing of the text is in the Early Han dynasty, in the second century BC. For a more specific date, we might look to 136 BC, when the *I Ching* was raised to the status of being one of the five 'Confucian classics'. It has also been pointed out that the *I Ching*, along with the other classics, was the subject of special study, sponsored by the government, as part of this process [37].

The other classics were the *Shu Ching* (Book of Documents), the *Shih Ching* (Book of Songs), the *Li Chi* (Book of Rites) and the *Ch'un Ch'iu* (Spring and Autumn Annals). A sixth classic, on music, has been lost. At this period, Confucianism was being established as the official philosophy of the state. As we shall see, this was also the period when the various commentaries surrounding the *I Ching* were being drawn together.

However, a distinction has to be drawn between the Han form of Confucianism and the teachings of its founder, K'ung fu-tzŭ (latinised as 'Confucius'), who lived c. 551-479 BC. Confucius was born in a period when the power of the Chou dynasty was in decline. Its territory had always been restricted to the northern half of the country, and at this point it only retained a nominal sovereignty over its domains. True power lay in the hands of the kings of a number of minor states, and China was beginning to fragment. The teachings of Confucius were intended to remedy this situation.

These teachings were basically of a moral and ethical nature. Religious and supernatural matters were avoided, as was the subject of cosmology. States were to be regulated by the correct observance of *li*, ceremonies and rituals. Family and human relationships were to be governed by *jên*, 'benevolence' or 'human-heartedness'. All this harked back to a supposed 'Golden Age' when the ancient social order was alleged to have corresponded with a natural moral order [38]. The rites to be observed were those in use at the foundation of the Chou dynasty; the exemplars of Confucian virtue were the ancient sages and emperors. Among these exemplary figures are such notables as Fu Hsi, King Wên and the Duke of Chou.

Confucius left his home state of Lu and travelled from ruler to ruler trying to promote this message. He was not listened to. The Chou dynasty lost more and more authority, and the two strife-torn centuries following Confucius' death are aptly known as 'The Warring States' period. Finally, in 221 BC, the western state of Ch'in overwhelmed all opposition and established the first truly country-wide empire.

The political turmoil of the Warring States period also coincided with the development of a number of contending philosophical schools, including Confucianism, Legalism, Taoism and the school of yang and yin. The Ch'in dynasty adhered to the Legalist philosophy and put its theories into practice. This resulted not only in a reliance on law, but in an authoritarian and totalitarian regime which ran the country primarily for the benefit of the state, rather than the people it contained. Ch'in Shih Huang-ti, the First Emperor, was intent on creating a new order and sweeping away the old. The Ch'in standardized weights and measures, the coinage, the characters in which Chinese was written, and so on; remarkable and lasting achievements for a dynasty that lasted only 14 years. It is thus no surprise that the founder of this new order was particularly averse to talk harking back to the golden days of antiquity and the superior virtues of the legendary sages and emperors. As the Confucians were particularly prone to talk of just such things, their writings were burned and their scholars buried alive. The *I Ching*, however, being a 'useful book' of divination, was spared the fires.

It may be well to point out here that by today's standards books would have existed in very few copies. Paper only started to come into use during the Han dynasty, and printing was not invented until the T'ang, some centuries later[39]. Books of the Han period and earlier were always hand-written, usually on individual slips of bamboo. These slips each held about 40 words. The slips were then strung together to make a 'scroll'. On rare occasions, books were written on silk. Such small numbers made it quite feasible to burn every copy in existence of a particular book. It also means that, with those books that survived, manipulation of the text would be comparatively easy.

After four years of bloody warfare following the fall of the Ch'in, the establishment of the Han dynasty in 202 BC marked a turning point. Attempts were made to recover the ancient literature and, more importantly, to interpret it under the new conditions prevailing under a relatively peaceful empire. The following four centuries were a hive of scholarly activity, and it is to this period that we must look for the writing of a large amount of commentatory material on all the classics. It was also the period when the texts of the classics themselves were edited.

This scholarly activity was not without its controversies, of course. One of these centred on the 'Old Texts' and the 'New Texts' of the classics. The New Texts were those assembled immediately after the fall of the Ch'in dynasty. These were written in the new characters introduced by the Ch'in and thus, because of their recent production, open to a certain amount of suspicion. The Old Texts were copies of the classics written in ancient (pre-Ch'in) characters, supposed to have survived the persecution and to be more reliable. Unfortunately, the circumstances in which some of these texts were 'found' seem somewhat dubious, so these texts are equally open to suspicion.

Around these two types of text developed separate schools of interpretation. The scholars of the Old Text school made their interpretations on the basis of the traditional Confucian morals and ethics. The New Text scholars were much more cosmologically inclined, their world-view being largely moulded by a non-Confucian background of yin-yang and Five Element theories, of which we shall have more to say shortly. The New Text scholars held the ascendancy in the Early Han period; but by the end of the Later Han they had been overhauled by the Old Text school. Theoretically, the *Chou I* had never been lost, and so should have been immune from all this scholarly disputation. However, with so much editing, interpreting and intellectual debate over the other classics, it would be unwise to be categorical about it having remained entirely untouched[40].

The cosmological ideas used by the New Text school are generally traced back to Tsou Yen (c. 350–270 BC) who, if not actually inventing the concepts of the Five Elements and the yang and yin, is thought to be responsible for gathering together and systematizing ideas that originated no earlier than the fourth century BC. Tsou Yen's writings were said to run to 100,000 words. Regrettably, all are lost, and our main source for the life and ideas of this character derive from a biography by the Han historian Ssu-ma Ch'ien[41].

A native of the state of Ch'i, Tsou Yen's interests were wide-ranging. He studied and wrote extensively on the transmutations of the yang and yin. He made inventories of China's mountains, rivers and valleys, its wildlife, agricultural productivity and rarities. He went on to develop a cosmography based on the number nine, in which China, consisting of nine provinces, was seen as only one of nine sub-continents that together formed one of nine major continents. By a similar process of reasoning from the known to the unknown, he studied the cycles of history, tracing events back to the most remote origins of things, before Heaven and Earth were created. Most importantly, he arranged the revolution and transmutation of the Five Elements, with particular regard to their cyclical relationship to history.

It is this last item that gave Tsou Yen and his school particular importance in the political field. They showed that the legendary Yellow Emperor ruled under the aegis of the Element Earth, the Hsia dynasty under Wood, the Shang under Metal, the Chou under Fire[42]. This meant that a ruler could align himself with the Element currently prevailing, making use of the symbolic colour attached to that Element and organizing his state according to the other Elemental correspondences. More importantly, when the Chou dynasty was in an obvious state of collapse, one who aspired to power could align himself with the Element that was rising to supremacy, Water, and which would ultimately replace the Fire of the Chou.

It is notable here that the cycle of Elements referred to is that of Destruction or Conquest, rather than of Generation. All the earliest surviving references to the cycle of the Elements are given in these terms, and it seems quite clear that the Destruction cycle is the earliest of the two.

The Ch'in dynasty accordingly took Water as its Element and black as its colour. But the extreme brevity of the Ch'in rule led to problems in the Han. If the Ch'in was a legitimate dynasty, then the Han should naturally take Earth as its Element and yellow as its colour. However, one school of thought regarded the Ch'in merely as a brief interregnum before the establishment of what was truly the new dynasty, the Han. In that case the Han should have taken Water as its Element and black as its colour. This dispute seems never to have been satisfactorily resolved, and undoubtedly led to the decline of the theory of correspondence between Elements and dynasties.

One reason why the dispute remained unsettled may be found
in the philosophical ferment of the times. It was at this point that
a new theory of cyclical interchange between the Elements came
into being: the cycle of Generation. In political terms, this naturally
gave a completely different interpretation to that of the Destruction
cycle. Previously, it was believed that the Fire of the Chou was
conquered by the Water of the Ch'in, and this in turn was conquered
by the Earth of the Han. According to the Generation cycle,
however, the Fire of the Chou would give rise to Earth for the Ch'in,
and this would then give rise to Metal for the Han.

The origin of the Generation cycle is generally dated to the
beginning of the Han dynasty[43]. We might speculate that it possibly
originated in an attempt to subvert the political propaganda of the
Ch'in, which used the Destruction cycle to establish its legitimacy.
This aside, in purely philosophical terms, it appears to have been
formulated in an attempt to match the Five Elements with the
transmutations of the yang and yin. Previously, the transformation
of these two principles had been thought to proceed by simple
alternation, from positive to negative and back to positive again.
Now, however, a third stage was introduced into the process; that
of equilibrium between the two. The yang and yin were then further
subdivided to give two stages of each principle, that of 'rising
growth' and 'maturity'. This resulted in a process of alternation
of five stages all told, which could then be correlated with the
Elements as shown in the following table[44]:

Yang	Rising Growth Maturity	Wood Fire
Equilibrium	Tranquillity	Earth
Yin	Rising Growth Maturity	Metal Water

Five is here rather more than merely the central number of the
of yang and yin. Earth, the Element of the centre, reasonably
correlates with the stage of equilibrium. Fire and Wood are naturally
connected, so it is easy to see why Wood was attributed to the 'rising
growth' stage of yang. The only 'forced fit' would appear to be

that of Metal. Nonetheless, it is easy to see how the sequence of the Generation cycle could be constructed from such an exercise in correlation.

The comparatively late date of all this material should perhaps be emphasized once more. There is no mention of the words yang and yin, or of the Five Elements, in the *Chou I*. Nor do the concepts appear in the Confucian *Analects* or *Mencius*[45]. There is an oft-quoted mention of the Five Elements in the 'Great Plan' chapter of the *Shu Ching* (Book of Documents)[46]. If authentic, this would take the origin of the Elements, though not their cycles, back to the beginning of the Chou dynasty. However, the chapter in question, along with several others, is now thought to be a forgery of the third century BC[47]. The use of the Five Elements seems to have reached full currency only in the same century.

Tsou Yen's followers did not survive long as a separate school. Instead, their basic theories, of the yang and yin and the Five Elements, became the common property of all the philosophical schools. In particular, they were used by the Confucian scholars of the New Text school; the Han cosmologists.

It may well be wondered why the *I Ching* should have been adopted as a Confucian classic, especially when Confucianism is considered in its original form, as a system of moral and ethical teaching. In fact, the early Confucians were not particularly interested in divination, strange phenomena, spirits, gods or ghosts. A famous passage from the *Analects* says: 'The subjects on which the Master did not talk were: extraordinary things, feats of strength, disorder and spiritual beings'[48]. His immediate followers were of like mind. This is not to say categorically that the early Confucians had no interest in divination; but the emphasis was elsewhere. Besides, the *Chou I* is not a moralizing text; what advice it does have to offer is generally of a purely practical nature. Indeed, there are even times when contradictions appear between the *Chou I* and the later 'Confucian' commentary appended to it.

As an example, let us look at the fifth line of hexagram 28, Preponderance of the Great. The original line judgement of the *Chou I* reads: 'A withered poplar puts forth flowers. An older woman takes a husband. No blame, no praise.' Here the text emphatically refuses to make a moral judgement. The commentary, however, reads: ' "A withered poplar puts forth flowers." How could this last long? "An older woman takes a husband." It is nevertheless a disgrace'[49]. In this case, at least, the *Chou I* is plainly in conflict with traditional Confucian virtues.

However, the *I Ching* as a whole was of use to the Han cosmologists of the New Text school. Of special interest to them was the corpus of commentatory material which was being assembled at roughly the same period, with its emphasis on the interchange of yang and yin and the cyclical progression of time. Not surprisingly, the date when the *I Ching* was elevated to the status of a classic, 136 BC, was also during the period when the New Text scholars were enjoying their greatest ascendancy. Once declared a classic, the *I Ching* retained its status until the present day; but its elevation is due to cosmological Han Confucianism, rather than to the earlier period of Confucius and his immediate followers.

Nonetheless, while the New Text scholars may have shifted the emphasis away from ethics towards cosmology, they were still Confucians. It was still necessary for them to show good grounds for taking in the *I Ching* among their canonical works and presenting 'the only true interpretation', rather than leaving the book as a common cultural property of all schools of thought.

Part of this process was the construction of the traditional history, tying the book in with the legendary sages and emperors. As founding fathers of the Chou dynasty and established Confucian worthies, King Wên and the Duke of Chou were obvious candidates for the attribution of authorship of the *Chou I*.

The involvement of Confucius with the book may have required deliberate fraud. In the standard text of the Confucian *Analects* (*Lun yü*) we read a quotation attributed to Confucius himself, which says: 'If some years were added to my life, I would give 50 to the study of the *I*, and then I might come to be without great faults'[50]. However, a more authoritative text for the *Lun yü* has now been found, in which the word '*I*' does not appear. In its place is another character of similar pronunciation meaning 'also' or 'even'. This quotation would thus read: '. . . I would give 50 to study, and then *even* I might come to be without great faults'[51]. With the change of only one word, the Confucian school managed to show that it had official sanction for the study of the *I Ching*.

The final part of this process consisted of the assembly of a corpus of commentaries showing how the book could be interpreted in a Confucian light. These interpretations covered the whole range of Confucian thought, both cosmological and ethical.

These commentaries are known as the Ten Wings. There are only seven texts, but three of them contain two parts, so the total is counted as 10. All are translated by Wilhelm and, for the most part, distributed throughout his edition under the hexagrams to which they refer. Unfortunately, this can lead the unwary to erroneously think that parts of the commentary, such as 'The Image', are actually part of the original text.

Wilhelm's own commentary, frequently in the form of 'Confucius says about this line . . ', is not particularly helpful either. In fact, the texts in question literally read 'The Master said . . ', and this is always *assumed* to be Confucius. However, it is well known that Confucius never actually wrote anything. Even such early texts as the *Analects* were written by his immediate followers, recording the sayings of the Master after his death. Certain of the commentaries are written in the same style but, as we shall see, these are so much later than Confucius that a direct ascription is hardly conceivable.

In dealing with the Ten Wings, it may be as well to divide the seven texts into two groups, of which the first can generally be considered the earliest. The first group consists of the following:

1. The *T'uan Chuan* (The Commentary on the Decision), parts one and two.

2. The *Hsiang Chuan* (The Commentary on the Images), parts one and two. This is an amalgamation of two texts, the *Ta-Hsiang Chuan* (Great Image Commentary), dealing with the hexagram as a whole, which Wilhelm gives in both parts of his translation as 'The Image'; and the *Hsiao-Hsiang Chuan* (Lesser Image Commentary) dealing with the individual lines of the hexagrams, which Wilhelm distributes throughout the latter part of his translation by line.

3. The *Ta Chuan* or *Hsi-Tz'u Chuan* (The Great Appendix), parts one and two.

4. The *Wên Yen* (The Commentary on the Words of the Text), the surviving part of which deals only with the first two hexagrams.

Dating these texts is difficult, and is made more so in the case of the *Ta Chuan* and the *Wên Yen* by the fact that they are very obviously compilations from diverse sources. The terms yang and yin are used in the *Ta Chuan*, and in fact this is the earliest text in which they do appear as philosophical concepts [52] ; but the Five

Elements do not. Neither of these sets of terms appear in the *Wên Yen*. It would, however, be unwise to argue from this that these commentaries must therefore be older than Tsou Yen (350 BC). The concepts of yang and yin and the Five Elements seem only to have been combined in the Han[53], and these commentaries may simply be the work of a school of thought that made no use of the Elements. On the other hand, the *T'uan Chuan* and *Hsiang Chuan* do make use of the Elements, if in a fairly rudimentary form. These commentaries can thus be fairly confidently assigned to a time after Tsou Yen. The *Ta Chuan* is probably the oldest of this group; the earliest date conjectured for its origin is the third century BC[54].

The second group of commentaries in the Ten Wings are:

5. The *Hsü Kua Chuan* (The Sequence).
6. The *Tsa Kua Chuan* (Miscellaneous Notes).
7. The *Shuo Kua Chuan* (The Commentary on the Trigrams).

The *Hsü Kua Chuan*, which explains why the hexagrams are arranged in the order we have them today, is obviously late. It cannot date before the standardization of the text as a whole. If the conjectured date for this, 136 BC, is correct, the *Hsü Kua Chuan* must date either from that time, or later. It would, for example, be quite inapplicable to the text found at Ma-wang-tui, dating from 168 BC. This subject is dealt with more fully in Appendix Two.

The *Tsa Kua Chuan* is so brief as to have very little importance. It refers only to the meanings of the hexagrams as a whole, and is written in extremely succinct verse. It possibly originates in diviner's notes, and may be intended as a simple mnemonic.

The *Shuo Kua Chuan* is generally admitted to be the latest of the commentaries, and from a Confucian point of view, the least canonical of all. Curiously, it is the most important of the texts to be dealt with in examining the relation of the trigrams with the Han cosmology. However, the non-canonical status of the *Shuo Kua Chuan* is illustrated by the fact that the philosopher Wang Chung (AD 27–97) described it dismissively as having been 'found by some woman from Heng'[55].

Dating the *Shuo Kua Chuan* is made more difficult by the fact that it consists of two separate texts. The text we have today consists of 11 sections, which Wilhelm divided arbitrarily into three chapters, with two sections in the first chapter, sections three to six in the second, and the remainder in the third. In fact, however, sections one to three are an independent unit. This was first suspected by Shchutskii in the 1920s[56], and has since been confirmed by the fact that a manuscript of these three sections was found amongst the material at Ma-wang-tui[57]. The remaining eight sections were not present. The first part of the *Shuo Kua Chuan* thus probably dates from the early second century BC; the latter part may date even as late as the first century AD.

As for the name, the 'Ten Wings', this only came into use during the Later Han dynasty, after AD 23. It therefore seems reasonable to assume that the entire corpus was not assembled in its final form until that date. As for the constituent parts, the most generally accepted dates are as follows:

The *Ta Chuan* (Great Appendix), *T'uan Chuan* (Commentary on the Decision), *Hsiang Chuan* (Commentary on the Images) and the first part of the *Shuo Kua Chuan* (Commentary on the Trigrams): end of the third, beginning of the second century BC.

Wên Yen (Commentary on the Words of the Text): second or first century BC.

Hsü Kua Chuan (The Sequence), *Tsa Kua Chuan* (Miscellaneous Notes), latter part of the *Shuo Kua Chuan* (Commentary on the Trigrams): late first century BC or early first century AD[58].

Only two of these commentaries give a treatment of the trigrams as separate entities, rather than merely components of the hexagrams: the *Ta Chuan* and the *Shuo Kua Chuan*. The former gives only a very embryonic treatment. Only in the latter part of the *Shuo Kua Chuan* do we find the fully developed system of attributes, arrangements and correlations which form the basic 'structural technology' of the *I Ching* system.

There was also another group of commentatory texts relating to the *I Ching*, written after 40 BC. These are the *I Wei* ('Apocryphal Commentaries on the Changes'), which formed part of a much larger body of literature known as the *Ch'an Wei* ('Oracles and Apocrypha')[59]. The *Ch'an Wei* as a whole provided apocryphal commentaries to all the classics, and were a product of the New Text school. With the decline of this school, the *Ch'an Wei* were eventually suppressed at the end of the Han dynasty. The *I Wei*, a collection of eight texts, is the only part of this literature to survive in more than fragmentary form. Regrettably, these texts have neither been translated nor studied properly, but it is possible to glean one or two items of information from the cursory studies that have appeared.

In summary then, the *I Ching* and its related cosmological system
is not as ancient as it first appears. It did not appear fully formed
at one single point in time, but has been put together from a number
of differing sources, of widely differing dates. The book we have
today is the result of a long process of accretion, the explanations
of the internal structure being the latest additions to the system.
Of particular importance is the fact that the trigrams themselves
were only invented late on in this process. They appear to be
contemporaneous with the other major elements of the correlative
cosmology, the yang and yin and the Five Elements. Lastly, this
cosmological system only reached its full development at the
beginning of the Han dynasty, early in the second century BC.
Before examining the trigrams in their true context, it is necessary
to turn our attention to that correlative cosmology and look at it
in more detail.

3
The Web of the World

Rightly or wrongly, we in the Western world of the twentieth century see the universe in a different way to that in which the thinkers of the Han dynasty saw it. Today, we have largely placed the description of the world in the hands of the scientists and this, rather than giving us a broad view of the world as a whole, has led to a narrow study of its individual parts. A major element of the scientific method is to remove a subject from the extraneous factors surrounding it so that it can be studied in isolation. The experimental chemist is, generally speaking, concerned only with the reaction taking place inside his laboratory vesssel; he has no concern with the weather outside the building, or if he has, it is to exclude such factors from his experiment. This tendency toward exclusionism is widespread. Disciplines have become separated; the micro-biologist and the mathematician have little to say to each other. Similarly, scientists in general have little common ground with artists or ministers of religion. We live in a world of specialization and differentiation, where even 'interdisciplinary studies' has become a specialised subject in itself.

In Han China, however, the universe was seen as one world, with all its parts linked together to make a single harmonious whole. The description of the world was in the hands of philosophers and cosmologists, and the emphasis was not so much on the study of the individual parts of the universe, but on interpreting how those parts related to one another as a whole. The 'tools' used in these interpretations were the Five Elements, yang and yin, the trigrams, numerology and the like. This system of correlations could perhaps be described as the 'scientific thought' of its day, but it was much more than that, the same techniques being applied also to politics, ethics, religion and so on. In fact, it offered a comprehensive key to the interpretation of everything in the universe.

While allowing for the differentiation of the individual parts of the universe, and of their actions, the emphasis of this system was placed on the similarity of those parts, and the way their actions balanced one another. As a simple morphological example, there might be mountains in one region and valleys in another, but high ground or low ground, it was still all ground and taken over all such differences would even out. Again, the two great cosmic principles match and give way to one another; when the yang advances, the yin retires, and vice-versa. When the sun rises, the darkness retreats, and when the sun sets, the darkness returns. If in summer the days are long and the nights short, then equally in winter the days are short and the nights long. The universe as a whole was seen to be striving to maintain just such a harmonious balance between all its parts.

Again, the Five Elements are balanced in that they have both a Generation and a Destruction order. Both these orders are cyclical; Wood may destroy Earth, but eventually, when the cycle completes itself, Wood in turn is destroyed by Fire. In either order, each of the Elements was thought to dominate over the others for a similar period of time, in the same way that the four seasons of the year are of equal length. Just as winter is succeeded by the other seasons, and the year is completed when winter returns, so time itself was thought of as being circular, rather than linear[1]. All things return to their own beginning, and the same thinking can be seen in the circular arrangements of the trigrams.

When dealing with the cyclical orders of the Five Elements, it is obvious that they must be treated more as processes than as physical substances. Considered as a process, each Element has two aspects. Wood is both a productive process which generates Fire, and a destructive one which conquers Earth; similarly for the other Elements. When the Generation and Destruction cycles are integrated together, the universe can again be seen striving for balance and not allowing one part to preponderate over the other. This is perhaps best illustrated by supposing a malfunction in the system, in which each of the Elements attempts to expand at the expense of the others. If there were to be an unusual preponderance of the Element Wood, this would eventually bring it into contact with Metal, which destroys it. However, Wood is also a process which gives rise to Fire, which destroys Metal. Metal, in turn, produces Water, which destroys Fire. Then Fire produces Earth, which conquers Water, and Water generates Wood, which conquers Earth. Earth, in turn, gives rise to Metal, which once again conquers Wood[2]. And so the cycle goes on, endlessly repeated in a harmonious whole.

As everything in the universe was thought to be composed of these Five Elements in various proportions, it is hardly surprising that attempts were made to correlate their substances and processes with the phenomena and processes of the everyday world. The most obvious correlation is that of Fire with summer and Water with winter. These correlations were then expanded to include the other seasons as well, according to the Generation cycle of the Elements: Metal was correlated with autumn, Water with winter, Wood with spring, Fire with summer. However, there are obvious problems here; there are Five Elements and only four seasons. This problem was never really resolved in any satisfactory way. There was one school of thought which gave the Element Earth to an indefinite period of late summer and early autumn, so keeping strictly to the order of the Generation cycle. Another, however, divided up the Earth 'season' into four separate periods of 18 days, and then inserted these between the other four seasons of 72 days each; thus giving a correspondence to the lunar year of roughly 360 days.

Similar problems arose with the four directions. Metal was attributed to West, Water to North, Wood to East, and Fire to South. Again, Earth was left over, and had to be attributed to a 'fifth direction', the Centre.

Obviously there was something very special about the number five which gave it sufficient importance that natural sets of four, such as the seasons and directions, had to be adapted to fit with it. One possible reason for this is the importance of the number five in the quinary arithmetic of the counting rods, discussed in the last chapter. There may, however, be more to it than that.

Cammann[3] has suggested that the number five is a symbol of centrality. Centrality was an important concept in ancient China; the land was, after all, known as the Middle Kingdom. It had been torn apart during the Warring States period and the desire for a strong central ruler was strong; a desire only fulfilled with any permanence in the Han dynasty.

According to Cammann, a major symbol of centrality is the magic square of three. In this the numbers one to nine are arranged in a square, three numbers to a side, so that each column adds up to 15, whether they are read vertically, horizontally or diagonally.

$$
\begin{array}{ccc}
4 & 9 & 2 \\
3 & 5 & 7 \\
8 & 1 & 6
\end{array}
$$

Five is here rather more than merely the central number of the arrangement. Multiplied by three, the base number of the square, it gives 15, the number of the totals. Multiplied by nine, the highest number in the square, it gives 45, which is the total obtained by adding all the numbers together. It is also the mean between the numbers on either side; for instance, five is half way between three and seven. These pairs on either side of five all add up to 10 (9 + 1, 3 + 7, 4 + 6, etc.), which divided in half gives five. It is also the number which falls in the middle of the series one to nine.

Cammann suggests that it is this emphasis on the number five, with its curious mathematical properties and its embodiment of the concept of centrality, which led to the classification of Five Elements, five directions, and so on. The magic square of three was known in China as early as the Warring States period, and it seems almost certain that it was known to Tsou Yen, the propounder of the Five Elements theory. It is also interesting to note that in his geographical speculations he divided China into nine provinces, arranged in a three-by-three square. It is thus highly probable that Tsou Yen used the magic square as the basis for his numerical and geographical ideas[4]. The square becomes, in fact, a diagram of an idealized China, divided into Nine Provinces with a strong central ruler represented by the number five. To its inhabitants, China was, if not 'the whole of the known world', then at least all of the Earth that was worth worrying about; an Earth which was believed to be square, in contrast to the roundness of Heaven.

Once started, this system of classification developed rapidly. Apart from the Five Elements and the five directions, we also find five colours, tastes, smells, musical notes, viscera, orifices, sacrifices, virtues, ancient rulers, mountains and planets. The lists could be extended almost indefinitely[5]. All these classifications by five were correlated one to another. Wood, for example, corresponded with East, spring, blue, sour, a goatish smell, the liver, the eyes, the planet Jupiter, and so on.

The end result was a beautifully patterned conception of the universe, with everything in its place and a place for everything. By that same patterning, everything was connected with everything else. This connection could be made directly, through classificatory correspondence (as in the connection Wood-blue-Jupiter, mentioned above), through shared yang- or yin-ness, or cyclically through the Generation and Destruction cycles of the Five Elements[6].

These classifications were also applied to the various types of ministers at court, the rules of their behaviour, and to the virtues in general. Ultimately man himself, being composed of the Five Elements in the same way that everything else was, could consider himself directly linked to the universe at large. The universe outside could affect him both physically and behaviourally, but similarly, he and his behaviour could affect the universe in turn.

The mechanism by which these effects were brought about was not thought of in terms of linear cause-and-effect. Tung Chung-shu (c. 179–104 BC), the major elaborator of this theory, gives two main explanations.

The first of these theories is that 'things of the same category activate one another'[7], or that like acts upon like. Tung argues his case by example. A neighing horse will be answered by another horse; a lowing cow will be answered by another cow. However, a horse will not be answered by a cow, nor a cow by a horse. Of two otherwise identical pieces of wood, fire will burn the dry one in preference to the wet one, because dryness is an attribute of fire, whereas wetness is in direct opposition to it. To a twentieth century mind, these particular examples may not seem convincing enough to construct a cosmology upon, but at least the general lines of Tung's thought are apparent.

Tung's second explanation, and by far the most important, was that of resonance. Let us assume that two identical lutes are similarly tuned and placed in the same room. If a particular note is struck on one lute, the second lute will produce the same note by resonance, without its being touched. To an observer with no knowledge of sound-waves, there is no direct visible cause for this effect. Reasoning by analogy, if this principle of 'action-at-a-distance' applies in one case, there should be no reason why it cannot work in other cases where similar forms or materials are involved. As the entire universe is made up of 'similar material' (in that it is all composed of the Five Elements), it thus becomes quite logical to assume that everything within it resonates one part with another, Wood with Wood, Metal with Metal; and man with the world at large[8].

The thought here is lateral rather than linear. The universe is seen as a vast interconnected web in which individual parts, although separated by distance, can still act upon one another, even though there is no direct connection between them either spatially or temporally. Without the necessity of a linear connection, resonance is seen as a simultaneous process.

This provides a functioning rationale for sympathetic magic, astrology, divination and similar 'pseudo-sciences'. Jupiter, known to the Chinese as 'The Wood Star', would resonate with terrestrial Wood, along with all the colours, tastes, smells, virtues and so on that are associated with it. As the Chinese constellations were cor-related with various areas of the country, the appearance of Jupiter in a particular constellation would thus affect the Wood Element in a particular region on the ground. The same correlative reasoning also provides a 2000 year old forerunner to the 'acausal connecting principle' posited by Jung under the name 'synchronicity' to explain meaningful coincidences[9]. To the Han mind, there simply was no such thing as 'coincidence'; all such events were merely functions of the patterned universe and its web of connections.

If mankind was seen as part of the universe, made of the same materials and in a relationship of resonance with the larger whole, this by no means reduced man's significance. Man was also seen to play a major role in another important concept, the trinity of Heaven, Man and Earth. On a cosmic scale, Heaven was naturally the most important part of this trinity, and was believed to be purposeful and desirous of peace, harmony and benevolence. These desires in no way indicate a personalized 'God'. It is simply a matter of nature seeking balance or harmony, and such harmony is obviously best attained in times of peace and benevolent rulers. On a day-to-day basis, however, Man was thought to play the most important role, for he had the greatest facility for direct action, be it for good or evil. By resonance, such actions would then draw responses from the universe at large. As Tung Chung-shu put it:

'The action of man, when it reaches the highest level of goodness or evil, will flow into the universal course of Heaven and Earth, and cause reciprocal reverberations in their manifestations'[10].

As Man's representative, it was the emperor who played the leading part in this trinitarian relationship and, by extension, his actions could seriously affect the running of the universe as a whole. If the emperor was virtuous and benevolent, if peace was maintained and the welfare of the people was given priority, then all would go well. However, an emperor of insufficient virtue would be displeasing to Heaven and Earth, whether that insufficiency was manifested in either weakness and a decline of the state, or in evil, hedonism and a proclivity for war. Similarly, if the nobles or officials were responsible for starvation, corruption or violence within the empire, the emperor would again be responsible, as the events were occurring within his domain. Either way, the trouble in the human world would cause an imbalance in the system, and draw a reaction from Heaven and Earth.

These reactions were usually in the form of 'anomalies and catastrophes'. 'Anomalies' were comets, solar eclipses, unusual appearances in the sky and so forth, and were taken as the first signs of Heaven's discontent. 'Catastrophes' were earthquakes, floods, serious fires and the like, and provided much stronger warnings. If these portents were not heeded Heaven would eventually bring the state to ruin, 'withdrawing its mandate' from the reigning emperor and bringing about his replacement by a new ruler, or even a new dynasty.

Similarly, a ruler of virtue and benevolence could expect to receive auspicious portents from Heaven. These, curiously, are much more rare and fantastic than the inauspicious portents. Among their number were appearances of dragons, phoenixes, nine-tailed foxes and mythical trees. There was obviously a certain political bias inherent in the system. The chief desire was to restrain the emperor from the excesses that his position as absolute monarch naturally allowed him[11].

This system of resonance was not a one-way affair, however. Man was also thought to be able to assist the operations of Heaven and Earth. When the sun was eclipsed, it was thought to be overwhelmed by the yin. It could be aided to recover its yang power by the beating of drums, as loud noises had yang characteristics which would help, in turn, to subdue the yin. Again, in times of

drought the southern gates of the city would be closed in order
to block off the direction from which the fiery influence came. At
the same time the northern gate would be opened, to allow the
watery influences to enter.

It was by ritual, particularly those rites carried out by the emperor
as mankind's representative, that most help could be given to
keeping the 'system' running in good order. There were various
books of rites, mostly dating from the early Han period, which
prescribed the correct and appropriate activities. The emperor was
thus supposed to wear robes of the colour linking with the current
season of the year, to face the appropriate direction for particular
actions, to have the correct music played on a particular occasion,
and so forth. All these prescriptions were designed to fit in with
the cosmic pattern and, by their correctness, to ensure the
continuance of the universe[12].

According to the manuals on the rites, the emperor was supposed
to carry out these major ritual functions in a special building known
as the *Ming T'ang*, the 'Hall of Brightness'. This building represented
a microcosm, a model of the universe in miniature. It is described
in the *Po Hu T'ung* (Comprehensive Discussions in the White Tiger
Hall). This is the record of a great debate between the scholars of
the Old and New Text schools over the interpretation of the classics,
and dates from the Later Han dynasty.

> 'The *Ming T'ang* is round at the top, and square at the bottom. It
> has eight windows and four doors. It is the building whence the
> orders of state proceed, and it is situated south of the capital. The
> top is round in imitation of Heaven, the bottom is square in imitation
> of Earth. The eight windows represent the Eight Winds, the four
> doors the Four Seasons, the nine compartments the Nine Provinces,
> the 12 seats the Twelve Months, the 36 single doors the Thirty-six
> Rains, the 72 window-openings the Seventy-two Winds'[13].

It should also be noted that the nine compartments representing
the Nine Provinces have been linked to the numerals of the magic
square of three. The building thus represents not only a symbolic
model of the real world over which the emperor ruled, but also
the magical/cosmographic idealized world of China. By carrying
out the appropriate rituals in the *Ming T'ang*, the emperor's rule
and virtue would radiate, by resonance, to every part of the empire.
A similar idea might be reflected in the fact that, ideally at least,

old Chinese cities were perfectly aligned with the cardinal points. So positioned, the rectangular walls would represent the square Earth. Order being correctly maintained within this miniature world of the city, the ruler's influence would thence reverberate into the surrounding countryside.

Any such microcosm would thus be of considerable importance. Perhaps it should be emphasized that we are dealing here not with a simple 'artistic symbol', but with something that has an active use. Be it large like the *Ming T'ang*, or small like the simple magic square of three, it is nonetheless a model of the universe, and linked by resonance to the world at large. At the highest level, the symbols are used in the imperial ritual which ensures the smooth running of the universe. At a more mundane level, which is how the system survived in the popular religion of post-Han times, microcosms can be used to perform magical operations of a personal nature [14].

In Chapter 1, mention was made of the fact that one of the charges brought against Liu An, the Prince of Huai Nan, was the treasonable possession of maps. The reasoning behind this charge should now have become more clear. The map was a microcosm of the territory it represented. As such, the map gave both symbolic and magical control over the territory shown [15]. The possession of a map would thus usurp the Imperial prerogative, and so could provide the grounds for a treason charge.

Perhaps the most startling example of the use of a microcosm in the Han period pertains to Wang Mang, the usurper whose reign (the Hsin 'dynasty', AD 9-23) divides the Earlier from the Later Han. A firm believer in the cosmological system discussed here, Wang Mang constructed a *Ming T'ang* to the south of the Han capital Ch'ang-an. This building has recently been excavated, and corresponds closely to the literary model [16].

At his overthrow, with the Han armies closing in and already burning the palace, he refused to flee. Instead he withdrew to the Hsüan Room, which seems to have had some special cosmic significance. There, dressed in deep purple and wearing the imperial seals at his belt, he sat with a 'Diviner's Board' before him. This, which will be discussed in more detail further on, was a microcosm consisting of a square Earth plate and a round Heaven plate.

The Heaven plate was mounted on a pivot above the Earth plate, and could be rotated. The Earth plate was inscribed with a number of directional and temporal symbols, such as the Ten Stems and

Twelve Branches. The Heaven plate was usually inscribed with
the stars of the Dipper (the major part of Ursa Major), although
in Wang Mang's model this may have been replaced by a magnet
in the shape of a ladle (again corresponding to the shape of the
Dipper), which was used to obtain compass directions. The board
was adjusted to correspond with the day and hour, and Wang Mang
turned his seat to co-ordinate its direction with the Dipper. He
remarked: 'Heaven has given the (imperial) virtue to me; how can
the Han armies take it away?' And there he sat, apparently con-
fident that by establishing himself in the symbolically correct
position he would be under divine protection. Alternatively, he
may have believed that by assuming such a position his imperial
virtue would be made manifest, and so would over-awe his
opponents. Either way, it made little difference. He was found still
sitting there by his enemies, who duly killed him[17].

Little mention has been made of the eight trigrams so far, but
naturally they fit into the same system. The trigrams have correlations with the directions, Elements, yang and yin, and so forth.
These relationships will be examined in more detail in the following
chapters. Beyond the most important correspondences which will
concern us there, the system was extended with the same sort of
near-infinite variation as that of the Five Elements. The trigrams
were correlated with the Eight Winds, the eight types of instru-
mental music, the eight parts of the body, and so on[18].

Of course, the circular arrangements of the trigrams are much
more than simple explanatory diagrams used in the interpretation
of the *I Ching*. They too are microcosms, used in ritual and magic.
They have an active part to play, rather than being simply objects
of philosophical contemplation. As the *Po Hu T'ung* says: 'He
(Fu Hsi) drew up the Eight Trigrams in order to rule all under
Heaven'[19]. Again, the *I Ching* as a whole is itself a microcosm,
containing all the possible combinations and fluctuations of the
yang and yin, and information about the situations arising
therefrom.

The Han practice of imperial ritual to regulate the cosmos has
passed away but, as we shall see, the trigrams are still used in the
rites of the Taoist religion. They mark the perimeter of the sacred
area, dividing it off from the world at large and leaving the Taoist
to practice his rites in a miniature universe of his own . . . a
microcosm[20].

The time has now come to examine these miniature worlds of the trigrams in more detail . . .

Part Two
Circles of Heaven and Earth

4
The World of the Senses Arrangement

There are two major arrangements of the eight trigrams and a third, more obscure one which will be dealt with individually in this and succeeding chapters. As was pointed out in Chapter 2, the trigrams and their arrangements were derived from the hexagrams at a comparatively late date. They were used in the interpretation of the pre-existing text of the *Chou I*, rather than the text being based on the symbolic attributes of the trigrams themselves.

The World of the Senses arrangement is also known as the sequence of Later Heaven, King Wên's trigrams, the Inner World arrangement, or the World of Phenomena. It is often said to be the later of the two major arrangements of the trigrams. This is probably because tradition attributes its invention to King Wên, whereas the World of Thought arrangement was attributed to the much earlier sage, Fu Hsi. Needham is of the opinion that these attributions to King Wên and Fu Hsi are very late, dating from the tenth or eleventh centuries AD[1]. In such a case, references of an earlier date to the trigrams 'of King Wên' or 'of Fu Hsi' would presumably refer not to particular arrangements, but simply to the trigrams in general. The references would only be to the inventors of the trigrams as such, and not a differentiation between varying sequences.

Regardless of when the arrangements themselves came into existence, the idea that the World of Thought is older than that of the Senses may well reflect 'Golden Age' thinking. The World of Thought arrangement is considerably more logical and symmetrical than that of the Senses, and 'backward-looking' Chinese thought would naturally ascribe the greatest posterity to the most perfect arrangement. However, the evidence seems to point to the opposite conclusion, that the World of the Senses is the older of the two arrangements, which is why it is being dealt with here in the first place.

The World of the Senses sequence is correlated with the compass points, and is arranged as in Figure 4. South is shown at the top, and the lowest lines of the individual trigrams are positioned toward the centre of the diagram.

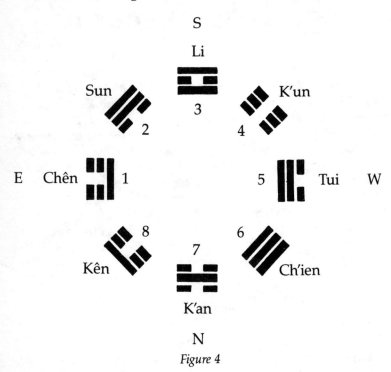

Figure 4

This is certainly the arrangement most commonly mentioned in works of the Han dynasty, if not the only one. It is also the sequence referred to in such commentaries as the *T'uan Chuan* (Commentary on the Decision) when directional attributes of the trigrams are used in the interpretation of the hexagrams. We also have archaeological evidence of its use in the Han period, as this sequence appears on a Diviner's Board which has been excavated from a tomb thought to date from AD 68[2]. Later Diviner's Boards continue to use the same arrangement, and the implication seems to be that if the World of Thought sequence was known at all at the time, it was not used in any directional sense.

There is, indeed, a suggestion that the World of Thought arrangement was not in use during the Han period at all. In the *History of the Three Kingdoms* a conversation is recorded between Kuan Lo (AD 209–256), a famous geomancer, and his friend Liu Fen. Kuan Lo said:

> 'I really do not understand why our ancient sages placed Ch'ien at the North-West and K'un at the South-West. After all, Ch'ien and K'un are the symbols of Heaven and Earth, the supreme things . . . How could these be reduced to the position of the other six trigrams? . . . How could they occupy side positions?' [3]

As a geomancer, Kuan Lo should have had a full knowledge of the arrangements of the trigrams. The implication here is that the World of Thought sequence (where Ch'ien and K'un are placed at the top and bottom of the arrangement) was unknown to him. A further implication would seem to be that the original logic behind the World of the Senses sequence had been forgotten, even at such an early date as the third century AD; otherwise Kuan Lo would have known full well why Ch'ien and K'un were placed in the North-West and South-West. The apparent lack of logic in the arrangement has been much debated. Regrettably, the commentatory material on the sequence is rather confused and unhelpful.

The World of the Senses is said to relate to the real, phenomenal world in which we live; the world perceptible to the senses. By contrast, the World of Thought is said to show the idealized interchange of yang and yin as cosmic principles. The Senses sequence is usually numbered from Chên in a clockwise direction, although it should be pointed out that nowhere in the Ten Wings are numbers actually connected with the individual trigrams. This numbering system has arisen simply from the order in which the trigrams are treated in the *Shuo Kua Chuan*.

The cardinal points are occupied by the trigrams Chên, East; Li, South; Tui, West; K'an, North. According to the *Ch'ien Tso Tu* (The Way Opened by Ch'ien), one of the apocryphal *I Wei* texts, these four cardinal trigrams are known as the Four *Chêng*, or 'uprights'. The remaining four, in the diagonal positions, are known as *Mên*, 'Gates' or *Wei*, 'Holders Together' [4].

The arrangement also shows the changing seasons of the year, Chên representing spring; Li, summer; Tui, autumn; K'an, winter. Following on from this seasonal cycle of growth and decay, it also demonstrates the life and death of plants, animals and mankind. The *Shuo Kua Chuan* has the following to say about this arrangement:

> 'God comes forth in the sign of the Arousing; he brings all things to completion in the sign of the Gentle; he causes creatures to perceive one another in the sign of the Clinging (light); he causes them to serve one another in the sign of the Receptive. He gives them joy in the sign of the Joyous; he battles in the sign of the Creative; he toils in the sign of the Abysmal; he brings them to perfection in the sign of Keeping Still'[5].

This passage is obscure, to say the least; so obscure in fact that the compilers of the *Shuo Kua Chuan* felt constrained to provide a commentary upon it in the section immediately following. Slightly abbreviated here, this says:

> 'All living things come forth in the sign of the Arousing . . . they come to completion in the sign of the Gentle . . . Completion means that all creatures become pure and perfect. The Clinging is the brightness in which all creatures perceive one another . . . The Receptive means the earth. It takes care that all creatures are nourished . . . the Joyous is midautumn, which rejoices all creatures . . . The Creative is the trigram of the North-West. It means that here the dark and light (yin and yang) arouse each other . . . The Abysmal means water. It is the trigram of due North, the trigram of toil, to which all creatures are subject . . . Keeping Still is the trigram of the North-East, where beginning and end of all creatures are completed'[6].

As Fung Yu-lan points out[7], no adequate explanation of these correlations is present in this text. He then goes on to quote another passage from the *Ch'ien Tso Tu*, which makes a little more sense of the sequence and ties it in more firmly with the cycle of the seasons. According to this, Chên, the Arousing, produces things, and is correlated to the second (lunar) month, which is approximately the beginning of spring. Sun, the Gentle (fourth month), disseminates them, as wind. Li, the Clinging (fifth month), as the sun gives them growth. K'un, the Receptive (sixth month), being earth, nourishes them. Tui, the Joyous (eighth month), harvests them. Ch'ien, the Creative (tenth month), puts them in good order. Kên, Keeping Still (twelfth month), marks their termination and beginning. Each trigram is said to cover a period of 45 days, and the eight make up a 360-day lunar year.

This explanation is a slight improvement. The idea that the trigram Sun disseminates things as wind is markedly better than that it brings them to completion, to take only one example. However, the explanation is still extremely arbitrary. If the primary purpose of the sequence was to explain the progression of the seasons, there is a serious problem in its logic. K'un, the major embodiment of the yin principle, has been placed in a position corresponding to late summer, while Ch'ien, the major embodiment of the yang, has been placed in early winter.

Perhaps a more reasonable theory would be that the passages given above reflect a rather desperate reasoning about an arrangement the purpose of which was not properly understood. As already mentioned, it has been remarked that the World of the Senses arrangement seems to be an arbitrary construction, without any logical or numerical basis. In fact, Blofeld goes so far as to say that: 'It is said in China that beings above the level of humans are able to discover the meaning of this order, whereas humans are no longer able to do so'[8]! This sounds rather daunting, but let us press on with the investigation.

According to the surviving literature, it is this arrangement in particular in which the Five Elements are attributed to the trigrams, as shown in Figure 5.

There are obvious problems in correlating Five Elements with eight trigrams. Once again there appears to be a certain arbitrariness about the process. The four cardinal directions are given their correct Elemental designations: East, Wood; South, Fire; West, Metal; North, Water. The Element Earth presents a problem, of course, as its direction is the Centre. The trigrams K'un, earth, and Kên, mountain, are obvious candidates to represent the Earth Element, but they have to be placed on the circumference of the circle, rather than at the centre. There is, though, no immediately apparent reason why they should have been placed on the South-West/North-East axis.

The linking of the trigram Li with Fire and the South seems quite natural, as does the correspondence of K'an with Water and the

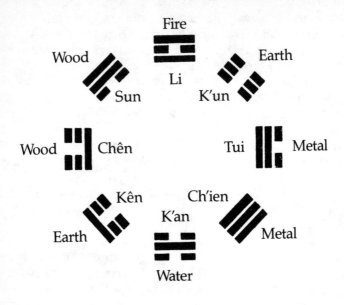

Figure 5

North. However, the remaining two Elements are again problemati-
cal. The *Shuo Kua Chuan* makes a strong correlation between Sun
and wood, but the correlation it gives between Chên and wood
is much weaker. Both trigrams are correlated with Wood in this
arrangement, but if the sequence had been drawn up in order to
show the directional co-ordinates of the Elements, it would be more
logical to expect Sun to be placed in the East, rather than Chên.

The metallic connections of Tui and Ch'ien are weaker still. The
Shuo Kua Chuan makes no mention of metal in connection with
Tui whatsoever, and metal is only listed as a minor attribute of
Ch'ien. This appears to be further evidence that the *Shuo Kua Chuan*
was written without a full understanding of the sequence it
describes. It is possible that the commentary merely records a pre-
existent correlation between Ch'ien and metal, while having nothing
to say about the reason for it. Indeed, as will be shown in Chapter
6, it seems quite possible that the entire collection of Elemental
designations of the trigrams first originated in a separate source.
They would then have been treated as 'accepted facts' and made

to fit with the World of the Senses; this would then explain the logical defects in their positioning.

Reading round from Chên in a clockwise direction, the Generation cycle of the Five Elements *almost* appears: Wood generates Fire generates Earth generates Metal generates Water generates Wood . . . except that Kên, Earth, is misplaced. This is an interesting 'near miss'; the fact that it is so nearly, but not quite, right may well suggest again that the primary purpose in drawing up the arrangement was not to show the Elemental correspondences of the trigrams. Some other purpose seems to have been in the inventor's mind when the arrangement was drawn up, to which the Elemental attributes were secondary.

The consequences of the 'misplacement' of Kên are interesting. Kên, apart from being the 'beginning and end of all creatures', lies in the North-East. In later Taoist religion, the North-East is thought to be the direction from which the demonic forces enter the world, and this area must be ritually sealed off before performing certain services in the temple[9]. It is tempting to speculate that one of the reasons why the North-East has gained this unfavourable reputation is because it is where the Elemental arrangement of the World of the Senses breaks down into imperfection; where the world is 'out of joint'.

A similar situation pertains to the familial attributes of the trigrams. These are usually said to be connected with the World of the Senses, and are arranged in two groups. The female trigrams run clockwise from Sun to Tui, the male from Ch'ien to Chên. However, within those groups there is no logic or symmetry. The female trigrams run as follows: eldest daughter, middle daughter, mother, youngest daughter. The male trigrams run: father, middle son, youngest son, eldest son. As with the Elements, it appears that the familial attributes were secondary to the primary purpose of the arrangement and may, again, derive from a separate source.

The World of the Senses arrangement is frequently connected with or superimposed upon the *Lo Shu* diagram. The Lo Shu, 'The Writing from the River Lo', is one of a pair of diagrams mentioned in ancient sources, the other being the *Ho T'u*, the 'Yellow River Chart'. The Ho T'u is connected with the World of Thought arrangement, and will be discussed in the next chapter.

According to legend, both the Ho T'u and the Lo Shu were 'heavenly gifts' to the mythical Emperor Yü the Great. The Ho T'u was brought by a dragon-horse which emerged from the Yellow (Ho) River, the Lo Shu by a turtle from the River Lo. Mentions of these gifts go back to the fifth century BC[10], but regrettably we have no idea exactly what the Lo Shu was thought to be in those early days. No diagrams have survived from that period, and it is possible that the Lo Shu was originally conceived of as a written text, rather than as a chart.

The Lo Shu as we possess it today is a Chinese representation of the magic square of three, which has already been discussed in relation to Tsou Yen. Literary descriptions, without illustrations, of the magic square and its connection with the trigrams go back to the Han dynasty, and are mentioned in the *I Wei*[11]. The actual diagram that appears today under the name of the Lo Shu, shown

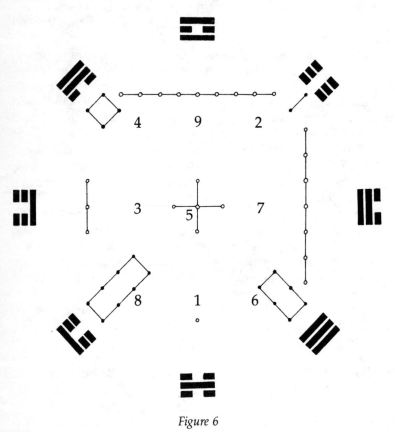

Figure 6

in Figure 6, can be dated no earlier than the Sung dynasty[12]. Here the numbers are represented as patterns of linked dots. Odd, yang numbers are shown in white and even, yin numbers in black. Whether the magic square of three was represented in the same fashion during the Han dynasty, or even if it was called the Lo Shu then, cannot be determined. There is, besides, a variant of the diagram, also called the Lo Shu and based on the magic square of three. This dates from the Sung dynasty as well, but is correlated with the third arrangement of trigrams, and will be discussed in more detail in Chapter 6.

Recently, John S. Major has shown a connection between the numbers of the Lo Shu and the Destruction cycle of the Five Elements[13]. It will be recalled that the Chinese considered odd numbers to be yang, even numbers yin. The basic source for this idea is the *Ta Chuan* (Great Appendix) commentary to the *I Ching*, where we read that 'Heaven is one, Earth is two, Heaven is three . . .' and so on, up to 10[14]. Also, in the 'Great Plan' chapter of the *Shu Ching* (Book of Documents), the Five Elements are given in the following order: first Water, second Fire, third Wood, fourth Metal, fifth Earth[15]. By combining these two systems and taking the numbers one to five as those by which the Elements come into being and six to 10 as those by which they are completed, we arrive at the following table:

1st	Heaven engendered Water
2nd	Earth engendered Fire
3rd	Heaven engendered Wood
4th	Earth engendered Metal
5th	Heaven engendered Earth
6th	Earth completed Water
7th	Heaven completed Fire
8th	Earth completed Wood
9th	Heaven completed Metal
10th	Earth completed Earth[16].

It will be noted that the Elements are here enumerated in an order which is neither the Generation nor the Destruction cycle. However, each Element is given a pair of numbers (for example, Water is 1 and 6) representing its birth and completion, which are also a yang and yin pair.

Major then proceeds to apply these numerical correspondences of the Elements to the magic square of three, replacing each number of the square with its Element, as follows.

4	9	2	M	M	F
3	5	7	Wo	E	F
8	1	6	Wo	Wa	Wa

Earth, lying at the centre, is a problem which prevents the reading of the arrangement as a circle. However, if this is taken into account, and the arrangement is then read in an anti-clockwise direction, the Destruction cycle of the Five Elements appears:

$$
\begin{array}{ccc}
M \leftarrow & M \leftarrow & F \\
\downarrow & & \uparrow \\
Wo & E & F \\
\downarrow \ \nearrow & \downarrow & \uparrow \\
Wo & Wa \rightarrow & Wa
\end{array}
$$

It should be noted here that the Elements attributed to the numbers in the magic square have no correspondence with the Elemental designations of the trigrams in the World of the Senses arrangement. Water and Fire both appear twice in the magic square, but only once in the trigrams, and there is no correspondence of position.

As mentioned previously, reading round the Elemental attributes of the trigrams in the World of the Senses, we *almost* have the Generation cycle of the Elements. If such was the case, we would have a neatly symmetrical arrangement: clockwise trigrams showing Generation around anti-clockwise numbers showing Destruction. With the other two arrangements of trigrams, to be discussed in the following chapters, such symmetries do occur; but the World of the Senses remains imperfect. Furthermore, we have still not discovered why the Elements are attributed to the particular trigrams. That such attributions are not drawn directly from the Lo Shu should be obvious.

We have seen that the material related to the World of the Senses arrangement is riddled with problems. The existence of the sequence as early as the third century BC can be surmised from its usage in the earlier *I Ching* commentaries, but by the time any attempt is made to 'explain' it (in the *Shuo Kua Chuan* and the *I Wei*) the original meaning appears to have been lost. The fact that there seems to be no numerical or logical basis for the sequence has caused many scholars to simply dismiss it as 'arbitrary' and to pass it over. Similarly, it has been pointed out that neither the Lo Shu nor the Ho T'u have any connection with the *Chou I* itself[17].

However, we do know that the magic square of three was associated with the World of the Senses arrangement in Han thought and religion, especially in the cult of the god T'ai I, the 'Grand Unity' or 'Supreme One'. Further details of this cult will be found in Appendix Three. Such arrrangements and correlations cannot simply be passed over as 'arbitrary' and neglected. Unless we are prepared to accept that such arrangements and diagrams appear on the backs of tortoises and the flanks of dragon-horses, we have to concede that someone arranged the trigrams in the World of the Senses sequence, and that someone attached the Lo Shu to the arrangement; and, furthermore, that they must have had their reasons for doing so. Besides, there are other ways of seeing the world (and constructing arrangements of trigrams to represent this world-view) which take little or no account of logic or numerology. This, I would venture to suggest, is what we have here; not a logical arrangement, but a mythological one.

That the explanation to be offered differs from those already given by no means negates them. The surviving interpretations already contain a number of different explanations for differing purposes: a geographical one related to the cardinal points; a demonstration of the life-cycles of nature; an annual time-progression in terms of the four seasons, and so forth. Fortunately, all these interpretations seem to be complimentary rather than contradictory. In short, there may be several answers to a single question.

When speaking of Chinese myth a certain amount of caution must be observed, because we are by no means talking about a simple or single unit. China is a vast country and has a number of minority nationalities with myths and traditions of their own. Furthermore, the majority Han nationality has spread over such a wide area that even among this relatively homogeneous group different traditions have sprung up in different places. Perhaps more important, China has a long history and her myth and religion have evolved over several thousand years, continuing to do so virtually up until the present day. When looking for mythological explanations for the World of the Senses sequence, we must exercise a certain amount of care in choosing material which was common to a large proportion of the population (particularly to the Han nationality), and also appropriate to the time period shortly before the Christian era.

Let us begin with the Lo Shu. That a connection between the nine provinces of China and the magic square of three can be traced back to Tsou Yen has already been established. In mythological terms, however, such a connection is traced to the legendary Emperor Yü the Great, who traditionally lived in the twenty-third century BC. Yü is supposed to have quelled the Great Flood of Chinese mythology, to have set the rivers in their right courses, and to have first divided China into nine provinces. His travels are recorded in the 'Tribute to Yü' chapter of the *Shu Ching* (Book of Documents)[18].

At the time, of course, China was considered to be 'all the known world'; the Earth itself. The Earth was thought to be square, and to be surrounded by the Four Seas; although it has been suggested that these 'seas' are not so much literal oceans as 'seas' of barbarians which surrounded the Middle Kingdom. As the land was considered to be square and divided into nine provinces, it is hardly surprising that the Lo Shu (or whatever representation of the magic square of three preceded it) became associated with the country, and consequently with Yü himself.

In later Taoist ritual, the connection between the land, the numbers and the legendary emperor is further emphasized in the ritual movements known as the 'Paces of Yü'. Performing this, the priest moves in a pattern which follows the 'magic line' of the square of three. To do this, he moves around the square in numerical order, from one to two, two to three, and so on up to nine. These are the 'paces', and are said to simulate the course that Yü took on his travels through the nine provinces[19]. The 'magic line' is shown in Figure 7, and further details will be found in Appendix Three.

Another correlation between the Lo Shu numbers and the land of China is provided by a fragment from a lost work of the Han dynasty called the *Chiu-kung ching* (the Classic of the Nine Halls). According to this the odd, yang numbers of the magic square were taken as representing the Five Sacred Mountains of China, while

Figure 7

the even, yin numbers were said to represent four rivers. The number one represented the mountain Hêng Shan in the North; three, T'ai Shan in the East; five, Sung Shan in the Centre; seven, Hua Shan in the West; nine, Huo Shan in the South. The rivers were: two, the San Chiang (Three Rivers) in the South-West; four, the Huai in the South-East; six, the (upper) Yellow River in the North-West; eight, the Chi in the North-East[20]. The mountains and rivers mentioned here are mainly placed in the north of the country, suggesting that the system was devised in the area of the Han dynasty capital cities, Lo-yang and Ch'ang-an. If the fifth central mountain is disregarded, it is noticeable that the remaining four are in the positions that correspond to the four cardinal trigrams in the World of the Senses sequence that the *I Wei* refer to as *Chêng*, or 'uprights'. The designation of the intermediate trigrams as *Mên*, 'gates', perhaps becomes more understandable if they are seen as 'passes' between the mountains.

Before offering an explanation of the World of the Senses arrangement, it is necessary to make a fairly lengthy digression to examine certain ancient Chinese myths. These fulfil both the conditions of being a product of the majority Han nationality and of being appropriate to the last few centuries before the Christian era. The main myth to be discussed here is that of Hsi Wang Mu, the Royal Mother of the West, and her consort Tung Wang Kung, the Royal Duke of the East. A number of other ancient myths will also be examined, relevant for their contributions to the world-conception commonly held at this period.

Hsi Wang Mu and her consort are but one of several divine pairs appearing in Han and pre-Han mythology. Among the others may be mentioned the Weaving Maid and the Oxherd[21], the moon-goddess Ch'ang Ô and the sun-god Hou I, and Nü Kua and her brother/consort Fu Hsi. Fu Hsi, incidentally, is a rather different character in popular myth to the literary figure of the sage emperor who invented the trigrams; he and his sister were occasionally portrayed with snakes' bodies. Most of these divine pairs seem to be, to a certain extent, embodiments of the yang and yin. As time progressed, and at the latest by the end of the Han dynasty, Hsi Wang Mu and Tung Wang Kung had come to represent the two great cosmic principles *par excellence* and had, indeed, subsumed to themselves several of the characteristics of the other pairs[22].

It is notable that in all these pairings it is the female partner who is by far the most important of the two. It is the Weaving Maid who is the daughter of the God of Heaven, while the Oxherd appears to be simply an oxherd. Ch'ang Ô is worshipped to this day as the goddess of the moon, while Hou I is remembered much more for his feats as a human archer, before his elevation to the position of sun-god. Nü Kua has considerably greater mythological importance than Fu Hsi, and we shall return to the main story concerning her shortly. An interesting stele[23], possibly of the third century AD, shows Fu Hsi and Nü Kua together as attendants on Hsi Wang Mu, and in their snake-bodied form. Here Fu Hsi holds a set-square, to measure the square earth. Nü Kua holds a pair of compasses, to measure the circular heavens. Nü Kua is thus obviously the 'heavenly' member of the pair, rather than Fu Hsi.

Another stele[24] connects Fu Hsi with the sun and Nü Kua with the moon, rather than Hou I and Ch'ang Ô. The sun and moon are naturally supreme symbols of the yang and yin, and solar and lunar attributes also appear, though less forthrightly, in the story of Hsi Wang Mu and Tung Wang Kung. Again, Hsi Wang Mu is distinctly the major partner in this couple. Tung Wang Kung appears to have been created as a later 'afterthought' to provide her with a consort and make the pair complete. Curiously, while Hsi Wang Mu remained an important deity for centuries to come, Tung Wang Kung seems to have sunk into insignificance after the Han dynasty[25].

We are fortunate in having a fairly large amount of material on Hsi Wang Mu, and are thus able to trace her development throughout the historical period in which we are interested. Readers seeking more details are referred to the work of Loewe[26] and, though less easily available, Cahill[27]. However, I must summarize briefly here. The earliest possible reference we have dates back to the Shang dynasty, where an oracle-bone inscription refers to sacrifices to the Western and Eastern mothers, Hsi Mu and Tung

Mu[28]. There is, however, nothing to indicate that Hsi Mu is identical to the later Hsi Wang Mu.

The earliest definite references we have to Hsi Wang Mu date from the fourth and third centuries BC. She is mentioned as having 'got the Tao' in the *Chuang Tzŭ* book[29], and there is a reference to her in *Hsün Tzŭ* as being the teacher of the Emperor Yü the Great[30]. The first detailed description of her comes from the *Shan Hai Ching*, the 'Classic of Mountains and Seas'. This work falls into three sections. The date of Chapters 1–5 is disputed, theories ranging from the fourth to the second centuries BC. Chapters 6–13 are thought to be a product of the Early Han dynasty, while Chapters 14–18 were added in the fourth century AD, at which point the whole book was edited and possibly revised[31].

The earliest reference to Hsi Wang Mu appears in Chapter 2. Here she is described as being human in form, with the tail of a leopard, the teeth of a tiger, dishevelled hair, and being highly skilled at whistling[32]. This last attribute may at first sight seem absurd, but the Chinese have a tradition of divination by the use of the pitch-pipes, and there may be more to this than meets the eye. Similarly, the imitation of bird-calls is a common shamanistic practice and, according to Soymie[33], Hsi Wang Mu's long and dishevelled hair identifies her as a sorceress. However, at this early stage she seems to have had few divine attributes, especially as her identification with a goddess of epidemics has been shown to be in error. In the *Shan Hai Ching* she is simply one among a number of minor deities. She lives in the far West, in the region of the mythical mountain, K'un Lun.

The earliest mention we have of the worship of Hsi Wang Mu occurs in a history written in the first century AD, the *Wu-Yüeh Ch'un-ch'iu*, 'The Springs and Autumns of (the states of) Wu and Yüeh'. According to this source, in the fifth century BC King Kou Chien of Yüeh raised altars in the western and eastern suburbs of his capital. The western altar was dedicated to Hsi Wang Mu, the eastern one to Tung Wang Kung[34]. No trace of any such worship appears in Ssŭ-ma Ch'ien's biography of Kou Chien, though in another chapter he does mention Kou Chien 'imitating the eight trigrams of King Wên' to defeat his enemies[35]. As already noted, 'the trigrams of King Wên' may not, in fact, refer to the World of the Senses in particular, but simply to the trigrams in general. Ssu-ma Ch'ien was writing at the end of the second century BC, so both these references are late and may be anachronistic, but such a linking of Hsi Wang Mu and the trigrams through the medium of Kou Chien is worth noting, at least.

It should perhaps be pointed out that the state religion of China at this time largely concerned itself with an impersonal deity, *T'ien*, 'Heaven' or *Shang Ti*, 'The Lord on High'. Both terms seem to be virtually interchangeable. Lesser divinities such as Nü Kua or even Hsi Wang Mu herself were much more the subject of popular worship. As such, information about their cults is not particularly well preserved in the official histories and literature. Of course, even when dealing with literary references from datable texts it must be remembered that they post-date the events to which they refer. So when we meet Hsi Wang Mu again in a much more fully developed form during the Han dynasty, this obviously implies a continued process of growth between the fourth and second centuries BC. By the Han period, further elements had entered the picture.

In the late third century BC the First Emperor of China, Ch'in Shih Huang-ti, had developed a strong interest in finding the secret of immortality. This interest centred on the mythical Isles of the Blest, which were believed to lie in the Eastern Sea and to be the home of the Immortals. With these islands we run into considerable confusion in the source material. There is variously said to be one island, P'êng Lai; or that P'êng Lai is an island with three peaks; or that there are three islands, of which P'êng Lai is only one. There is similar confusion over the term Fu Sang. This can be either a divine tree which grows on P'êng Lai, a tree which grows on the shore of a vast continent lying beyond P'êng Lai at the other side of the Eastern Sea, or the name of that Eastern continent itself. While these difficulties have to be noted, for the purpose of developing our argument, we shall refer to P'êng Lai as a single island, and Fu Sang as the tree growing on it. P'êng Lai, as a mountainous island in the Eastern Sea, is taken as an analogue of Mount K'un Lun in the far West[36].

Interest in the Isles of the Blest seems to have peaked in the reign of the Han Emperor Wu Ti (r. 140–87 BC). He was also interested in the search for immortality, and during his reign a number of maritime expeditions were sent out. Unfortunately neither islands nor immortality were discovered. In a state of some disillusionment, Chinese eyes turned toward the far West. It was also in the reign of Wu Ti that the famous traveller Chang Ch'ien made his expedition westwards, an epic journey that lasted from 138 to 126 BC. Travelling through the heart of Central Asia, he journeyed as far as Bactria and so opened up the famous trade route known as the Silk Road. It was a measure of Hsi Wang Mu's importance at this time that Chang Ch'ien was moved to ask the Persians that he met about the goddess. These gentlemen apparently informed him that Hsi Wang Mu lived even further west in a land called T'iao-chih, although they had never seen her themselves. T'iao-chih has tentatively been identified as Mesopotamia[37].

Although the exact details of the process are unclear, by the Han dynasty Hsi Wang Mu had been elevated from the position of a minor deity to that of a major goddess. It was also thought that the peaches of immortality grew in her realm. Thus she was seen as holding the means of acquiring immortality and being a major channel for communicating with heaven[38]. Her popularity continued to grow throughout the first century BC, reaching its peak in 3 BC with the outbreak of a mass millenial movement centring around her. Hsi Wang Mu's appearance in the world was expected daily, and thousands of fanatics worshipped her with services, dancing and the exchange of talismans[39].

From about the same time there is a considerable increase in the number of iconographic representations of Hsi Wang Mu among the archaeological finds. Her popular cult seems to have remained strong and widespread until the second century AD, when it was somewhat superseded by the Buddhist and Taoist religions. However, Hsi Wang Mu continued to be a major deity in the Taoist pantheon throughout the first millenium AD, especially in the Mao Shan sect, and her history and iconography during this period has been traced in some detail by Cahill[40]. Exactly when Tung Wang Kung was united with Hsi Wang Mu to make a balanced pair is not clear, but it seems to have been no later than the beginning of the first century AD, and was probably earlier.

It is obvious that Hsi Wang Mu was reaching the peak of her popularity at about the time period in which we are interested, and indeed she seems to have been the major figure on the religious scene. It is now time to turn our attention to the mythical geography of the world in which she was worshipped.

One of the major cosmological myths known to have been in

existence during the time period which interests us features Nü Kua. She acts alone in this story, and it might be noted in passing that the earliest reference we have to her being paired with Fu Hsi is found in Liu An's *Huai Nan Tzŭ*, dating from the second century BC[41].

According to this myth, the heavens were supported on eight pillars. Other references give the number of pillars as four, but in either case they probably represent the directions. A being named Kung Kung, who is described either as a horned monster or a rebellious minister, contended with the mythical Emperor Chuan-hsü for the throne. Traditionally, Chuan-hsü reigned in the twenty-fifth century BC. Having been defeated, Kung Kung hurled himself against Mount Pu Chou. This mountain was the north-west pillar supporting heaven. The pillar broke and the sky collapsed, tilting toward the North-West, while at the same time the earth slipped toward the South-East. This explains why the rivers in China generally run toward the South and East; why the stars move toward the West; and why the pole is in the North rather than directly overhead, as it would have been expected to be if China was the central land under heaven[42].

Nü Kua's involvement in the story may well be a later development, or a separate story that has become attached to the first. She is said to have repaired the sky, which seems to have been partially shattered in the catastrophe, with stones of five colours melted together. Here 'five colours' could mean simply 'multi-coloured', but there may also be a reference to the Five Elements[43].

Another early cosmological myth relates to the sun and moon. According to this, the sun rises from the eastern island of P'êng Lai, where the giant Fu Sang tree grows. Each morning, the sun climbs up the branches of the tree before making its way westwards across the sky. At the end of the day it plunges into a lake, Yü Yüan, at the western extremity of the world in the K'un Lun mountains. The moon, on the other hand, first appears in the western sky when it is new. It follows the same path as the sun, but starts its journey from the western lake, appearing further East at every sunset as the month progresses[44].

Moving on to the myth of Hsi Wang Mu and Tung Wang Kung in its fully-developed form, we find this lake and island motif appearing once again. Tung Wang Kung lives on a paradisiac island in the Eastern Ocean, although in the early texts details of his realm are largely lacking. Large numbers of mulberries grow there, and the connection with the Eastern Element of Wood is obvious. Tung Wang Kung is also known as Mu Kung, 'The Wood-Duke'. This island is the home of Immortals, and is analogous to P'êng Lai or the Isles of the Blest in general. In a slightly later Taoist text written in the early centuries AD, the *T'ai-shang Lao-chün chu-kung yü-li*, we find that Tung Wang Kung's home is definitely stated to be P'êng Lai. For the purposes of developing a simple mythological geography, we can take Tung Wang Kung's home as being this island, which is a corresponding eastern partner to the western mountain K'un Lun, where Hsi Wang Mu lives[45].

In some early texts, Hsi Wang Mu is said to live *next* to K'un Lun rather than upon it, and the North-West is sometimes mentioned as her abode. In later versions, however, her palace is actually *on* K'un Lun, at the foot of which was the Jasper Lake[46]. K'un Lun seems in many ways to correspond to the Buddhist Mount Sumeru, the central mountain of the universe, although it held this position in Chinese texts long before the official introduction of Buddhism in 65 AD. It must be distinguished, however, from the range of mountains shown on present-day maps as 'K'un Lun'. These mountains were named *after* the mythical peak by the Han Emperor Wu Ti, at the end of the second century BC[47].

This is a very suggestive arrangement: a lake (a small amount of yin) amongst mountains (extreme yang); and a mountainous island (a small amount of yang) amongst a vast sea (extreme yin). We can also note another reversed symmetry. Hsi Wang Mu, the embodiment of yin, lives in mountainous yang territory, while the yang Tung Wang Kung lives in the yin ocean. One is reminded

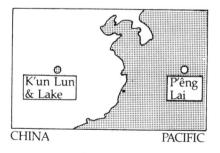

Figure 8

of the well-known T'ai Chi symbol, where yang and yin are represented as swirling 'commas', each containing the 'seed' of its opposite where its own concentration is greatest. This is graphically shown in Figure 8.

Hsi Wang Mu and Tung Wang Kung were said to be personifications of the yin and yang respectively, having been condensed from the quintessence of the Western and Eastern air[48]. The moon and sun are also frequently mentioned as personifications of the yin and yang, and Hsi Wang Mu and her consort also seem to have lunar and solar aspects. They both appear in the tale concerning the deities of these two luminaries.

Ch'ang Ô, the moon goddess, started out in a much more lowly position as the daughter of the god of the Ho, the Yellow River. This river was previously mentioned as lying in the North-West, when the numbers of the magic square of three were correlated with the mountains and waterways of China. Ch'ang Ô married Hou I, a famous hero and archer who was, incidentally, a close friend of Yü the Great and the royal forester at the time[49]. Once again we have a connection between the male member of the pair and the Element Wood. Hou I gained his connection with the sun in a separate tale, according to which there were originally 10 suns. These took turns to climb the Fu Sang tree and cross the sky on each day of a 10-day week. On one occasion, however, they decided to all come out at once, burning the earth when they did so. Nine of them were shot down with arrows by Hou I, leaving only the one that crosses the sky today. When the suns hit the ground, their bodies were found to be those of monstrous crows, and a bird is still associated symbolically with the sun[50].

After his marriage to Ch'ang Ô, Hou I built a palace for Hsi Wang Mu on Mount K'un Lun, and was rewarded by her with a gift of the pill of immortality. Ch'ang Ô stole and ate this, becoming immortal and flying to the moon. Hou I, going in search of her, arrived at Tung Wang Kung's palace and was there told of her whereabouts. He was afterwards immortalized and became the god of the sun. Hou I and Ch'ang Ô are said to meet only once a month, at new moon, when the sun and moon are in conjunction. A similar tale of regularized but infrequent meetings is told of Hsi Wang Mu and Tung Wang Kung. Hsi Wang Mu is said to visit her husband once a year, crossing from West to East over the back of a giant bird known as Hsi Yu, 'Seldom Seen'. This bird is said to span the world from

Figure 9
Top: Hsi Wang Mu in her late and fully-humanized form. Bottom: Ch'ang Ô,
the moon goddess. Ch'ing dynasty woodblock prints, by the Wu school.

West to East, sheltering Hsi Wang Mu and Tung Wang Kung under its outspread wings[51]. We seem to be dealing with almost identical pairs of deities here, under different names.

Hsi Wang Mu was also known as Chin Mu, the Golden Mother or Mother of Metal, and also as the Golden Mother of the Tortoise. The tortoise is the symbolic animal of the North, although Hsi Wang Mu's tiger teeth and leopard tail would seem to connect her with the tiger, the symbolic animal of the West. As said, Tung Wang Kung is less fully developed. The fruit of the mulberries in his island bestow immortality in the same way as the peaches of Hsi Wang Mu[52]. There seems to be no direct connection between him and a symbolic animal, although we might note in passing that the palace of the Dragon Kings of the Sea was also thought to lie in the Eastern Ocean.

Having assembled this large quantity of mythological material, it is now time to apply it to the World of the Senses. It has been shown that this was thought to be a horizontal arrangement, related to the cardinal points. As has also been said, the Chinese regarded the Earth as square and Heaven as round. When the circle of trigrams is placed round the square diagram of the Lo Shu, we have an extremely suggestive emblem. The Lo Shu can now be seen to represent the nine provinces of the known world, while the eight trigrams represent the circular heaven. This, it might be suggested, is the reason why the Lo Shu has been attached to the World of the Senses, rather than because of any numerical or Elemental connections.

However, the eight trigrams might also be seen as representing the eight pillars that hold up the sky. If the trigrams are regarded as an octagon, a shape 'half-way' between a square and a circle, the arrangement becomes more suggestive still. The trigrams would then be seen as lying in that borderland between Heaven and Earth, between life and death, between man and the gods. They are at the extreme edges of the world, half in and half out of the world we know, and might even be thought of as bridges between the realms of the mortal and the immortal. Hsi Wang Mu and Tung Wang Kung, holding the keys to immortality, likewise act as mediators between the terrestrial and the celestial. Their homes are in exactly this edge-of-the-world region, half in and half out of the world we know. Such a region is also the realm of a highly mythicized geography.

We have seen that, according to the myths, the earth tilted up toward the North-West and down toward the South-East. This means that it would swing on an axis lying across the North-East/South-West diagonal. Turning to the World of the Senses arrangement, we find that this same axis is also that on which lie the two trigrams with the Elemental designation of Earth, K'un and Kên. Earth being the Element attributed to the Centre, and these trigrams also meaning earth and mountain respectively, they make a neat unit across the middle of the arrangement. If this unit were now 'removed' from the reckoning as representing, at least in part, the world we know, then cosmologically the arrangement would start to make a lot more sense. This first stage is shown in Figure 10.

To begin with, the four remaining Elements are still represented by their trigrams in the correct cardinal distribution, Fire in the

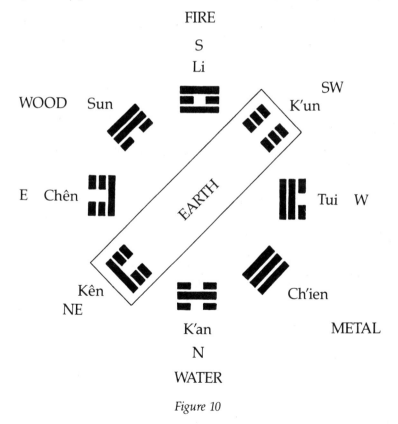

Figure 10

South, Metal in the West, Water in the North and Wood in the
East. The arrangement also starts to show more symmetry when
we divide it into yang and yin halves across the same axis. In
Chapter 2 we examined the way the Generation cycle of the
Elements was constructed to match with five phases of the
interchange between the yang and yin. There the 'rising' yang
corresponded with Wood, the 'mature' yang with Fire. Similarly,
'rising' yin corresponded with Metal, 'mature' yin with Water.
Earth, representing equilibrium, lay between the two yang and
yin halves. A similar structure presents itself here. Equilibrium is
represented by the two Earth trigrams, lying on the North-
East/South-West axis. To one side of this lie the two trigrams of
Wood, the rising yang, to the East and South-East, with the trigram
of Fire, the mature yang, to the South. We have seen that Sun has
a much greater association with Wood than Chên. Reading
clockwise then, the rising yang grows in strength from Chên to
Sun, then reaches maturity at Li. On the opposite side is a
symmetrical correspondence. The two trigrams of Metal, the
rising yin, lie in the West and North-West, with the trigram of Water,
the mature yin, in the North. Again, Ch'ien is more strongly
associated with Metal than Tui, so once more we have the rising
yin growing in strength from Tui to Ch'ien, then reaching maturity
at K'an.

Another curious fact about the arrangement was pointed out
by the Ch'ing dynasty scholar Ch'ên Mêng-lei[53]. Let us now look
at the trigrams as opposite pairs, as shown in Figure 11. Here we
find that K'un and Kên are in equilibrium, sharing the same
Element, Earth. However, the Element of K'an, Water, destroys that
of Li, Fire. Likewise, the Element of Ch'ien, Metal, destroys that
of Sun, Wood, and similarly for Tui and Chên. In short, the
Elements of the trigrams in the yin half of the diagram all destroy
the Elements of their opposite trigrams in the yang half. Why this
should be so is unclear; it may simply be coincidence. On the other
hand, we have seen that in the pairs of deities discussed above,
the female (yin) partner is the more important. Perhaps this is
reflected here in the destructive power of the Elements corresponding to yin.

It might be thought that this Elementary correspondence with
the rising, mature and equilibrious phases of the yang and yin
was sufficient explanation for the construction of the arrangement.

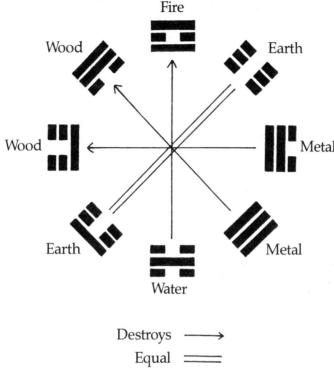

Destroys →

Equal ═══

Figure 11

Nonetheless, it still does not explain the directional placing of the individual trigrams. However, by developing the idea of yang and yin halves of the world further, we can see the mythical geography beginning to fall into place. We might even talk of the earth-axis dividing the arrangement into two 'realms', that of Hsi Wang Mu and Tung Wang Kung respectively. It is now time to look at the trigrams of these realms in terms of the myth and geography outlined above. We shall begin with the 'realm of Hsi Wang Mu'.

Tui in the West represents a lake. Its structure is that of one yin line (water) surmounting two yang lines (height), which could thus suggest 'a lake among mountains'. As the *Shuo Kua Chuan* informs us[54], Tui is a female trigram, representing a sorceress, and refers to the lips and tongue. Its Element is Metal/gold. Hsi Wang Mu is known as the Golden Mother, has the attributes of a sorceress and is good at whistling, and lives among the western K'un Lun mountains in close proximity to a lake. This is also the region of Yü Yüan, the lake where the sun sets and the moon rises.

The sky is said to tilt down closest to the earth in the North-West, which is where the trigram Ch'ien, Heaven, is positioned. We have seen that Hsi Wang Mu is also said to reside in the North-West, next to the mountain-and-lake complex represented here by Tui, in the West. Ch'ien is a Metallic trigram meaning heaven, and the Golden Mother as goddess of immortality also serves as a link to heaven.

K'an, although placed in the North, represents the moon. This obviously balances against the positioning of the sun in the South, but the moon also has traditional associations with the West. Hsi Wang Mu's lunar connections have been discussed above. The physical moon in the sky was thought to be composed of water, ice or crystal. K'an means water as well as the moon, and this watery element gives it another connection with the lake from which the moon is supposed to rise, represented here by Tui. The symbolic animal of the North is the tortoise, and Hsi Wang Mu is known as the Golden Mother of the Tortoise, as well as having connections with the Western tiger.

Here, then, are a collection of symbolic attributes relating to the trigrams which appear to link well with the mythology of the time, and those same trigrams are directionally linked with the accompanying mythical geography. In the Generation cycle of the Elements, Metal gives rise to Water. If we read round the trigrams in the same clockwise order from Tui, it is possible to see them as a sort of shorthand description: the western *lake* of *heaven* from which the *moon* rises, proceeding toward the *mountain* (Kên) which lies in the Eastern sea.

After this, we arrive at Chên and the realm of Tung Wang Kung, where a similar pattern presents itself, and a similar cycle begins. Even if it were to be argued that Tung Wang Kung is too late a development to be applicable to this arrangement, the apparatus connected with him (the island of P'êng Lai, the Fu Sang tree, the solar myths, and so on) was certainly current at a sufficiently early date.

Chên has one yang line under two yin lines, a reasonable symbol for an island *in* the sea, and correctly positioned in the East. It is the inverse opposite of Tui, the eldest son as opposed to Tui's youngest daughter. One of its attributes is the commencement of growth, and its Element is Wood. P'êng Lai was noted for the mulberries growing upon it, and Tung Wang Kung was known as the Wood Duke. P'êng Lai was also known as the 'Island of the Vase'[55], and the shape of Chên,☷, has been likened to a bowl[56]. The symbolic animal of the East is the dragon, and the *Shuo Kua Chuan* connects this animal with Chên[57]. As we have seen, the palace of the Dragon King of the Sea is also placed in the Eastern Ocean.

The next trigram, Sun, also has Wood as its Element. Besides this, wood is independently a major attribute of this trigram. It is tempting to see this as the Fu Sang tree growing on the island of P'êng Lai. The *Shuo Kua Chuan* associates Sun with the cock[58]. There is a story, possibly late, that Hou I came to the palace of Tung Wang Kung in search of Ch'ang Ô and was there given the Bird of the Sun. This was a heavenly cock which perched in the branches of the Fu Sang tree and announced the rise of the sun[59].

Li is, of course, the sun itself, thus connected with the East and South and having Fire for its Element. Li means weapons and sometimes more specifically arrows[60], the weapons of Hou I, the divine archer. The animal of the South is a bird, and the *Shuo Kua Chuan* again records a connection between Li and the pheasant[61].

The attributes of these trigrams again appear to link well with the myth and geography. In the Generation cycle Wood gives rise to Fire and in the same way the sun rises from the Fu Sang tree. Reading round the trigrams clockwise from Chên gives us another shorthand description: an Eastern *island* on which stands the *tree* from which the *sun* rises, travelling over the *earth* (K'un) toward the West, and the same *lake* from which the moon rises.

This seems to provide a neat explanation for the arrangement; an explanation which appears to have been forgotten and to have dropped out of the surviving literature. Such a mythological/geographical interpretation as this has considerably more internal logic than the commonly-quoted 'explanation' from the *Shuo Kua Chuan*, given at the beginning of the chapter, which should now appear to be quite indefensible.

In conclusion, the major cosmological points about the World of the Senses arrangement can be summarized as follows. It can be seen as a horizontal diagram arranged according to the compass-points. It demonstrates the life-cycles of nature. It contains an annual time-progression in terms of the four seasons. Arranged round the Lo Shu, representing the square Earth, it represents the circle of Heaven. It also appears to represent the borderland region of mythical geography, with its associated deities. It pertains to the daily motions of the sun and the monthly motions of the moon, and to the mythical geography associated with these motions. In contrast with the Lo Shu, which contains the complete Destruction cycle of the Elements, the World of the Senses shows some influence from the Generation cycle, but does not represent this cycle perfectly.

5
The World of Thought Arrangement

This arrangement is also known as the Sequence of Earlier Heaven, the Before the World arrangement, the Primal arrangement, or Fu Hsi's trigrams. It is perhaps the best known sequence of the trigrams, and is shown in Figure 12.

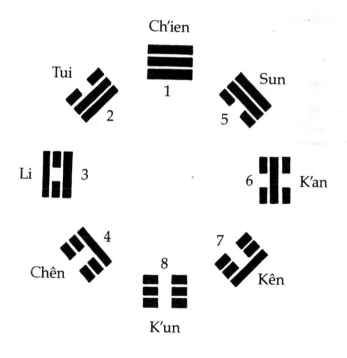

Figure 12

It will be noted that all the names given to the arrangement imply that it has priority to the World of the Senses sequence. As pointed out in the previous chapter, this is unlikely. The attribution to Fu Hsi need no longer detain us, and the sequence is not mentioned in any text before the Han dynasty. Beyond this, it becomes extremely difficult to say anything definite about the dating of the arrangement. Opinions vary by as much as 1200 years, from as early as the Han to as late as the Sung.

The argument for a Han origin depends on the apparent description of the arrangement in the *Shuo Kua Chuan*, the Commentary on the Trigrams. This passage can be dated to about the second century BC, as it appears among the fragmentary manuscripts found at Ma-wang-tui[1]. It reads as follows:

> Heaven and earth determine the direction. The forces of mountain and lake are united. Thunder and wind arouse each other. Water and fire do not combat each other. Thus are the eight trigrams intermingled.
>
> Counting that which is going into the past depends on the forward movement. Knowing that which is to come depends on the backward movement. This is why the Book of Changes has backward moving numbers[2].

The usual interpretation of this difficult passage is that it refers to the World of Thought arrangement, presumed to be already in existence at the time the commentary was written. The first paragraph refers to the fact that the trigrams can be arranged in pairs that are opposed in structure, each pair containing, in the total six lines, three yang and three yin lines. This can be seen, for example, in the pair Tui ☱ and Kên ☶. There is no mention of a circular arrangement, and nothing to suggest that such pairs are arranged opposite to one another in a particular sequence. In fact, the pairs of trigrams are not given in the same order as they appear in the World of Thought arrangement. Using the numbers normally attached to this sequence, the order of the pairs in this passage is 1 & 8, 2 & 7, 4 & 5, 3 & 6.

In the second paragraph quoted, 'that which is going into the past' is taken as referring to the yang 'decomposing' into the yin, the active principle becoming passive, and thus 'depending on the forward movement'. Reading round both halves of the arrangement in order, one to four, then five to eight, we find that in each series the yang lines become fewer, the yin greater, as we reach the higher numbers. 'That which is to come' is taken as referring to the yang growing out of the yin, the passive becoming active, and thus 'depending on the backward movement'. Again, reading round both halves of the sequence in the reverse order, eight to five, four to one, the yin lines become fewer, the yang greater.

This interpretation of the reason why 'the Book of Changes has backward moving numbers' seems to depend on the idea that all 'becoming' is to be taken as a movement from yin to yang, from passive to active. This one-directional notion seems rather to violate the cyclical philosophy of the *I Ching*, which sees change and the passage of time in terms of *both* growth and decay.

Such minor doubts about the correlation between the *Shuo Kua Chuan* passage and the World of Thought arrangement could easily be cleared up if we possessed an early example of the trigram sequence. Regrettably, we do not. The commentaries on the *I Ching* originally contained no diagrams; or at least none have survived which can be securely dated to the same age as the composition of the text. When visual representations of the Thought and Senses arrangements appear, they have been added at a later date, in similar fashion to the Lo Shu and Ho T'u diagrams. Such representations generally start to appear in the Sung dynasty, with the advent of large-scale block printing. Besides this, we have seen in the previous chapter that the World of Thought sequence was apparently unknown to the geomancer Kuan Lo in the third century AD.

The major problem, however, rests on the numbering of the trigrams in this sequence. In examining this question we arrive at the other end of the range of opinion regarding the dating of this arrangement. According to this theory, the World of Thought sequence is a product of the Sung dynasty. Ch'ên T'uan (c. 906–989 AD) is said to have 'transmitted the "Diagram of What Antedates Heaven" ' (that is, the World of Thought arrangement) to a number of followers culminating in Shao Yung (AD 1011–1077)[3]. It is to be noted that Ch'ên T'uan is only said to have transmitted the diagram, rather than to have invented it, and it is possible that he may have had access to a diagram of somewhat greater antiquity. However, Ch'ên T'uan is a shadowy figure about whom very little is known, so it is impossible to make definitive statements on the subject. As he was the founder of a particular school of interpretation, it is equally possible that the work of his later followers was also attributed to Ch'ên T'uan. All this aside, the theories of Ch'ên's school were given their definitive form by Shao Yung, and it is to his work that we must turn our attention in our search for clues.

Shao Yung is known to have been responsible for the circular arrangement of the 64 hexagrams. This is basically an expansion of the World of Thought sequence of the trigrams, using the same logic in its construction. Shao Yung also did a great deal of analytic work on the trigrams and hexagrams, drawing up diagrams to show their development, by division, from the original yang and yin. That for the trigrams is shown in Figure 13.

☐ YANG

▨ YIN

Figure 13

A similar diagram with six levels shows the evolution of the hexagrams, but that need not concern us here. The lowest section of the diagram shows simple yang and yin, and may be represented in *I Ching* terms as follows:

—— and – –

The second level from the bottom shows the yang and yin divided, and when this level is added to the first we obtain the 'Four Emblems':

═   ⚏   ⚎   ⚏

The top level divides again, and these sections being added to the two former levels, we arrive at the eight trigrams:

☰	☱	☲	☳	☴	☵	☶	☷
1	2	3	4	5	6	7	8

When this sequence is divided in half and placed in a circle, we have the World of Thought arrangement, and thus the numbering attached to it is explained. The implication here is that if the diagram showing the evolution of the trigrams from the yang and yin is attributable to the school of Ch'ên T'uan and Shao Yung, then presumably the World of Thought is also to be attributed to the same school[4]. This would mean, in effect, that the sequence of trigrams had been drawn up later than the *Shuo Kua Chuan*, and then fitted to the appropriate passage of the text; rather than the text describing an arrangement already in existence.

Such reinterpretations of the ancient commentaries by scholars of the Sung dynasty are not unknown. Shih-Chuan Chen[5] has described a similar case regarding the method of consulting the *I Ching* with yarrow stalks. The original yarrow stalk method was described in the *Ta Chuan*, the Great Appendix. This method of consultation was largely superseded by the use of three coins in the Sui and T'ang dynasties, and as a result was forgotten. The yarrow stalk method was re-invented by Chu Hsi (AD 1130-1200). However, as the original method had been forgotten, Chu Hsi was forced to reinterpret the text of the *Ta Chuan* to bring the procedure there described into line with the numerical procedures of the coin oracle. In doing so, he manipulated the text of the *Ta Chuan*, transposing certain paragraphs from their original positions. Chu Hsi's text of the *Ta Chuan* has since become the standard version, and is that which is translated in all the English editions. Similar Sung dynasty editorial work could conceivably be responsible for attaching the World of Thought arrangement to the passage from the *Shuo Kua Chuan*.

If the numbering system of the World of Thought sequence is, in fact, as late as the Sung, then these numbers could not have been applied to the trigrams when the *Shuo Kua Chuan* was written. If the trigrams had no numbers to run forwards or backwards, the interpretation of the *Shuo Kua Chuan* passage starts to look rather dubious. We shall have to examine the possibility that it may not refer to the World of Thought at all.

We have already seen that the first paragraph of the passage could

simply refer to pairings of trigrams of opposite structure. The basis
for making such pairings could just as easily originate in the familial
attributions of the trigrams. Ch'ien and K'un are Father and Mother,
Tui and Kên are youngest daughter and son, and so on. Again,
however, the pairs are not given in order. They read Father and
Mother, youngest children, oldest children, middle children.

More important, though, is the second paragraph with its
forward and backward moving numbers. As we shall see in the
next chapter, an equally forced explanation could be made which
relates the passage to the third arrangement, the World of the
Elements, which also has the trigrams arranged in opposite pairs.

However, it is quite possible that this passage does not refer to
the trigrams at all. As mentioned in Chapter 2, the *Shuo Kua Chuan*
consists of a combination of two separate texts, sections one to three
and sections four to 11. The passage under discussion is section
three, and thus has to be examined in relation to the first two
sections, which discuss the hexagrams rather than the trigrams.
Misleadingly, Wilhelm's translation places section three at the
beginning of an arbitrary 'Chapter 2', and thus relates it to the
following sections, which discuss the trigrams.

Let us examine the final paragraph of section two, which
immediately precedes the passage in question. This reads: 'The
places are divided into the dark and the light. The yielding and
the firm occupy these by turns. Therefore the Book of Changes
has six places, which constitute the linear figures' [6].

The important point to note when examining these two passages
is the phrasing. 'The Book of Changes has six places, which
constitute the linear figures'. And, again, 'The Book of Changes
has backward moving numbers'. The trigrams are not mentioned
as having backward moving numbers, but the Book of Changes;
and the Book of Changes has six places. Could it be, then, that
it is the hexagrams which have backward moving numbers?

In a hexagram, the lines are numbered from the bottom upwards;
the first line is the lowest place, the second above it, and so on.
The 'direction of movement', from the beginning of a situation until
its end, is upwards. Chinese texts were, of course, originally written
vertically rather than horizontally, from top to bottom. Such being
the case, an arrangement of numbers that placed six above five,
five above four, and so on, would naturally appear to be 'backwards'. The movement upwards in a hexagram ('that which is

to come') would therefore use a 'backward movement' of numbers. The reverse ('that which is going into the past') would thus use a 'forward movement'.

All this cannot be taken as positive proof that the *Shuo Kua Chuan* is not referring to the World of Thought sequence, of course; but it does raise serious questions. This is not helpful to our attempt to date the arrangement. There are arguments in favour of an origin dating to both the second century BC and the eleventh century AD; equally, there are doubts about both dates as well.

However, there is a vestigial form of the World of Thought arrangement which can definitely be dated to the Later Han dynasty. This appears in an extremely complex system which ties in six of the eight trigrams with the phases of the moon and the Ten Celestial Stems. The Stems are correlated with the compass points, and these correlations are attributed to Ching Fang (77–37 BC)[7]. They are as follows:

1.	Chia	East
2.	I	East
3.	Ping	South
4.	Ting	South
5.	Wu	Centre
6.	Chi	Centre
7.	Kêng	West
8.	Hsin	West
9.	Jên	North
10.	Kuei	North

The correlations between the Stems, the trigrams and the lunar phases appear in two texts, both apparently of the Han dynasty. The first is an abstruse alchemical text called the *Ts'an T'ung Ch'i* (known in English as 'The Akinness of Three'; the 'Three' being alchemy, Taoism and the *I Ching*). The *Ts'an T'ung Ch'i* is said to have been written by Wei Po-yang in AD 142. However, virtually nothing is known of Wei Po-yang historically, and the text may be slightly later. The other text is more secure. It is a fragment of a commentary on the *I Ching* by Yü Fan (AD 164–233). The texts are so similar that it is obvious that one has been derived from the other, and as Yü Fan's handling of the problem is slightly the more refined of the two, it seems likely that the *Ts'an T'ung Ch'i* is the earlier text. However, this is not really important. The fact is that the system decribed in both texts can be dated to the Later Han period.

In this system[8] the motions of the moon are correlated with the Celestial Stems, and its phases with six of the trigrams. On the third day of the lunar month, the new moon appears for the first time, and at sunset it first appears in the West. It is thus correlated with the Stem *Kêng* (West). On the eighth day it first appears at sunset in the South, and is correlated with the Stem *Ting* (South); and so on. At the same time, on the third day, the light of the moon is just starting to appear, and this is represented by the trigram Chên, ☳. Here the light is represented by the yang line 'entering' the bottom of the trigram while the greater part of the lunar face, still in darkness, is represented by the yin lines. On the eighth day the moon is half full and is represented by Tui, ☱. When the two systems are integrated together, the full set of correlations is as follows:

Third day (of the lunar month): the moon appears in the sky for the first time during the month. It is waxing and only slightly illuminated, and appears in the West at sunset. It is correlated with the trigram Chên and the Stem *Kêng*.

Eighth day: half full and still waxing, the moon appears at sunset in the South. It is correlated with the trigram Tui and the Stem *Ting*.

Fifteenth day: the moon is full and appears in the East at sunset. It is correlated with Ch'ien and the Stem *Chia*.

Sixteenth day: the moon now starts to wane, and this 'eating away' of the light is symbolized by the return of the yin lines, pushing up into the trigrams. At the same time, the emphasis on the direction of the moon switches away from its point of appearance at sunset to its point of disappearance at dawn. At dawn on the sixteenth, the moon disappears in the West. It is thus correlated with the trigram Sun and the Stem *Hsin*.

Twenty-third day: the half-moon, waning, disappears at dawn in the South. It is correlated with Kên and *Ping*.

Twenty-ninth (or thirtieth) day: the moon's light disappears. It is in the East at dawn, and is correlated with K'un and *I*.

These correlations can be summarized briefly in the following table:

Day of month	Stem	Direction	Trigram	Lunar phase
3	Kêng	W	☳	1st appearance
8	Ting	S	☱	1st quarter
15	Chia	E	☰	Full
				Waxing

				Waning
16	Hsin	W	☴	Starts waning
23	Ping	S	☶	Last quarter
30	I	E	☷	Darkness before New Moon

Here we have six of the trigrams used to represent the waxing and waning of the moon and the interchange of the yang and yin. They are given in the same order as that in which they appear in the World of Thought sequence, reading round clockwise from Chên. The trigrams Li and K'an are omitted. This is perhaps not surprising, as their structure would make it difficult to represent a phase of the moon with either of them. They are said, however, to correspond to the Stems *Wu* and *Chi*, the direction of which is the Centre. K'an and *Wu* are said to be the essence of the moon; Li and *Chi* the essence of the sun. The sun and moon are the great emblems of the yang and yin and, as purely celestial bodies, their relationship is responsible for the visible lunar phases. As such, they are said to control the whole process from the centre position, corresponding to *Wu* and *Chi*.

This still leaves the Stems *Jên* and *Kuei* to be accounted for. These Stems represent the North, where the moon never naturally appears. Here we have variant solutions. According to the *Ts'an T'ung Ch'i*, *Jên* and *Kuei* are equated with Ch'ien and K'un, which again are major symbols of the yang and yin, like the sun and moon. It explains this by saying that, as we have already seen, Ch'ien and K'un go with *Chia* and *I*, and that *Chia* and *I* in turn match with *Jên* and *Kuei*. However, this is given as a simple statement of fact, and no further explanation is offered[9].

Obviously hoping to avoid this repetition, Yü Fan offers the following explanation: between the thirtieth of the first month and the third of the following, the sun and moon meet at *Jên* and

disappear at *Kuei* (both in the North), and they then move to the
Centre, represented by *Wu* and *Chi*, before starting the cycle once
more[10]. Both these solutions seem rather inadequate, but they are
all that is offered to explain the discrepancies between the trigrams
and the Stems.

What remains uncertain, of course, is whether this correlation
between the phases of the moon and the trigrams was derived from
the World of Thought arrangement, or whether that sequence was
later constructed from the work of Wei Po-yang and Yü Fan. With
regard to the latter possibility, it is known that the *Ts'an T'ung Ch'i*
was known and appreciated by both Ch'ên T'uan and Shao Yung.

In summary, there are three possible time-periods that may be
suggested for the invention of the World of Thought arrangement:

1. The period shortly before the composition of the early material
in the *Shuo Kua Chuan*: no later than the early second century BC.

2. The period of Wei Po-yang and Yü Fan: second or third
centuries AD.

3. The period of Ch'ên T'uan and Shao Yung: tenth and eleventh
centuries AD.

It seems impossible to say more than this with certainty, although
personally I would favour the middle date, at the end of the Han
dynasty. This is purely a matter of opinion, however, and the
question must be left open. Putting aside the matter of dating, let
us move on and examine the structure of the World of Thought
arrangement.

This sequence is said to show the interchange of yang and yin
as great cosmic principles or abstract ideas; an idealized form as
opposed to the material world of everyday reality shown by the
World of the Senses. A parallel idea might be that of idealized
Platonic forms, existing in eternal perfection outside our normal
conceptions of time and space, but reflected in the world we know.
In some forms of interpretation the World of Thought arrangement
is said to 'shine through' that of the Senses. Thus Ch'ien, the major
embodiment of yang, is said to 'shine through' from its position
in the World of Thought to Li, the sun, in the World of the Senses,
by reason of their occupying similar positions. Similarly, K'un, the
yin, 'shines through' K'an, the moon. Other correspondences are
less satisfactory. This seems again to reflect 'golden age' thinking,
based on the mistaken idea that the World of Thought had priority
to the World of the Senses.

The trigrams are arranged in complimentary pairs of opposites. Thus Li, opposite in structure to K'an, is also placed in a position opposite to it, and this applies to all the pairs of trigrams. The opposition is complimentary, however: each pair of opposite trigrams contains, in total, three yang lines and three yin lines.

Apart from demonstrating the polarity of the cosmic principles, the arrangement also shows how yin changes into yang and yang into yin, in much the same way that the trigrams are used to reflect the waxing and waning of the moon. Movement in a trigram is upwards, starting at the bottom (innermost) line. The growth of the yang principle thus starts in Chên, where a yang line 'enters' the trigram in the lowest position. The same problem which led to Li's omission from Wei Po-yang's lunar system applies here also, of course. In this case, the problem is solved by saying that the lowest (first) line of the trigram is the most important, the second less important, the top least so. In terms of importance, then, the top line represents a smaller increment than the second. The next stage of growth after Chên is thus to have one yang line below a yin one, and a yang line above this, as in Li. The third stage comes with Tui, with two yang lines occupying the more important lower positions. The topmost yin line here is said to be about to be 'pushed out', as the growth completes itself in Ch'ien, which is entirely yang. In numerical terms, the sequence might roughly be equated with 1, 1½, 2, 3. The yin principle grows from Sun to K'un in a similar fashion, though an equally valid way of looking at it would be to say that the yang is decomposing into yin, being eaten away from below.

The World of Thought sequence is connected with the Ho T'u diagram, in the same way that the World of the Senses is connected with the Lo Shu. Once again, the Ho T'u diagram as we have it today, and as shown in most editions of the *I Ching*, is a product of the Sung dynasty. Both this and the Lo Shu have been attributed to Ch'ên T'uan[11]. The standard form of this diagram, with the numbers represented by linked patterns of dots (odd numbers white, even black), is usually shown with the World of Thought trigrams, as in Figure 14.

Even so, there are variants to this diagram. Figure 15 shows another Sung dynasty version of the Ho T'u, from the *I Ching Chên Ch'üan*[12]. Here the format is basically the same as in Figure 14, though the numbers are represented by stars, and not

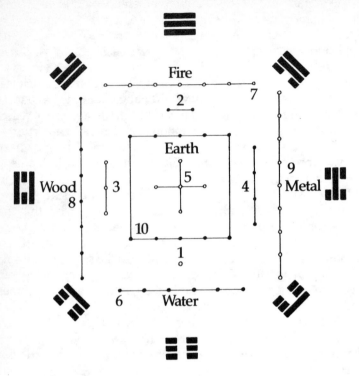

Figure 14

differentiated into odd and even, yang and yin. The names of the directions are given at the cardinal points, along with the written characters for the trigrams in the World of Thought arrangement. The diagonal texts read 'First diagonal occupied by Kên' and so on, and the trigrams occupy the correct positions, although the numbering of the diagonals appears curious. They are: first, Kên (lower right); second, Tui (upper left); third, Chên (lower left); fourth, Sun (upper right). The accompanying text provides no explanation for this order. However, the numbers of the Ho T'u are arranged in only four axes from the centre, while the trigrams occupy eight radial directions. If we take the numbers 1, 2, 3 and 4 in the Ho T'u and rotate their positions by 45 degrees anti-clockwise, they then occupy the same positions as the numbers mentioned in the diagonal texts.

Figure 15

The Ho T'u is thought to be later than the Lo Shu, the result of a revision of the emphasis of the world view which replaced the importance of the centre with an interest in the cardinal points; and here the numbers are arranged in a cross-formation, rather than a square[13]. However, the date of composition of the Ho T'u is again uncertain. Although it appears in relation to the World of Thought sequence, nothing can be inferred from this when the date of the World of Thought is so questionable.

The Ho T'u is mentioned by name in the same ancient sources as the Lo Shu. However, while we know that the magic square of three existed in some form during the Han dynasty, there is considerable disagreement as to what was the ancient form of the Ho T'u. Suggestions offered include a chart showing the twists and turns of the Yellow River (that is, a geographical map), an

unspecified arrangement of trigrams, or a type of jade sceptre[14].
The earliest reference to the numbers of the Ho T'u as we have
it today occurs in a fragment of a lost *I Ching* commentary
attributed to Kuan Lang, who lived in the fifth century AD.
However, the authenticity of this passage has been questioned also,
and the suggestion has been made that it dates from the eleventh
century AD[15].

When we examine the structure of the Ho T'u, we find that it
has a much more obvious connection with the Five Elements than
was immediately apparent in the Lo Shu. As pointed out in the
last chapter, pairs of numbers were attributed to each Element:
one and six to Water, two and seven to Fire, and so on. In the Ho
T'u, each of the five directions (centre and four cardinal points)
is represented by a pair of numbers, one odd, one even. The pair
of numbers attributed to each direction correlates with its Element.
One and six (Water) lie in the North; two and seven (Fire) lie in
the South; three and eight (Wood) in the East; four and nine (Metal)
in the West; five and ten (Earth) in the Centre.

The Ho T'u is also occasionally shown as a round diagram, rather
than a square one. This is supposed to show its heavenly qualities,
as opposed to the earthly qualities of the square Lo Shu. When
shown thus there is no basic alteration to the structure. The central
square, number 10, is simply shown as a circle and the outer lines
are curved to fit round it.

Whether round or square in format, we can note the development of two spirals of odd and even numbers within the Ho T'u,
each emerging from the central section representing Earth, as
shown in Figure 16.

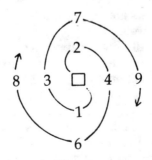

Figure 16

If we now look at the Ho T'u simply in terms of the Five Elements, a similar spiral appears, showing the Elements in the order of their generation: Earth giving rise to Metal, Metal to Water, and so on through the sequence, as in Figure 17.

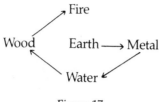

Figure 17

John S. Major has also tackled the problem of the Generation cycle in the Ho T'u[16], although his approach is somewhat more complicated. For some reason not clear to this author, Major has inverted the Ho T'u so that North appears at the top. In dealing with his material here I have reverted to the original for the sake of consistency, with South at the top. Major first shows the Ho T'u in purely numerical form:

$$
\begin{array}{ccccc}
 & & 7 & & \\
 & & 2 & & \\
8 & 3 & 10/5 & 4 & 9 \\
 & & 1 & & \\
 & & 6 & &
\end{array}
$$

He then goes on to convert this into a square diagram similar to the Lo Shu, with the odd numbers at the cardinal points, the even numbers at the diagonals, by rotating the even numbers 45 degrees anti-clockwise:

$$
\begin{array}{ccc}
2 & 7 & 4 \\
3 & 10/5 & 9 \\
8 & 1 & 6
\end{array}
$$

Major finally replaces the numbers with the Elements to give the Generation cycle, reading clockwise, in a similar format to his treatment of the Lo Shu, shown in the last chapter:

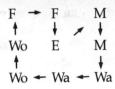

Such an interpretation shows an interesting symmetry with the Elemental structure of the Lo Shu. It also has the advantage of showing the Generation cycle as a closed process, constantly repeating itself, whereas a simple spiral structure leaves the process open-ended. However, if we return to the spirallic interpretation, we find another correlation with the World of Thought sequence. This can also be considered as a double-armed clockwise spiral, with the yang moving upwards and outwards from Chên to Ch'ien, the yin moving up and outwards from Sun to K'un. Again, in the Ho T'u, the transcendant Tao which generates the cosmos is said to lie at the centre of the diagram, at the central dot of the cross representing the number five[17]. Such a concept fits well with the idea of spirallic generation.

As each Element in the Ho T'u has a yang and yin (male and female) number, in popular tradition each Element is said to be represented as a 'married' pair, and thus to be able to 'give birth' to the next Element in the Generation cycle. The numbers one to 10 represent a complete cycle, and the Ho T'u is thus seen as a symbol of blessing, productivity and good fortune. However, the Lo Shu, having only nine numbers, is not a complete cycle, and the 'married' pairs are also broken. The Lo Shu is thus said to be a diagram incapable of generation, and to be one of change leading ultimately to death[18]. Here we may well have a popular interpretation of the fact that the Ho T'u contains the Generation cycle of the Elements, and the Lo Shu the Destruction cycle.

When looking at the World of the Senses arrangement in relation to the Lo Shu, we noted that the trigrams were directionally oriented, although the Elements of the Lo Shu were not. On the basis of reverse symmetry, we might expect that as the Elements of the Ho T'u are directionally oriented, the trigrams of the World of Thought would not be. However, the World of Thought trigrams are frequently shown with directional attributes. Such a directional orientation may derive from a desire to show the arrangement in the same format as the World of the Senses. Alternatively, it may have arisen from the arrangement's connection with the directionally oriented Ho T'u. Whatever the reason, this directional orientation certainly dates back to the Sung dynasty and, as we have seen, appears in the *I Ching Chên Ch'üan*[19]. This similarity of directional interpretations may also explain why the World of Thought is said to 'shine through' the World of the Senses.

However, there is no basis for any such directional attribution in the ancient commentatory material. The *Shuo Kua Chuan* gives directional attributes only to the World of the Senses arrangement. Such an interpretation may well be late and not intended by the original creators of the World of Thought sequence, for there is another way of looking at the arrangement. This is to regard it as being arranged in a vertical plane, rather than a horizontal one, with Ch'ien at the zenith and K'un at the nadir, as in Figure 18.

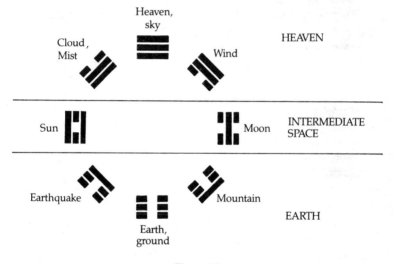

Figure 18

It will be noticed that the trigrams Li and K'an, representing the sun and moon, have been separated out as being bodies moving in the intermediate space between heaven and earth. It will be recalled that the lunar-phase system of Wei Po-yang and Yü Fan omitted these two trigrams also. Once these two trigrams are removed from consideration, the arrangement falls into two definite sections, and it will be immediately apparent that there is a preponderance of yang (heaven) lines in the upper section, and of yin (earth) lines in the lower. Taken together, Li and K'an have an even distribution of yang and yin lines between them, which provides another reason for omitting them from this division.

In the upper, yang section there are three trigrams whose meanings connect them with the sky: Tui, meaning rain, cloud or mist, Ch'ien, the embodiment of heaven itself, and Sun, wind. Similarly, the lower, yin section contains earth-oriented trigrams: Kên, mountain, K'un, the embodiment of earth, and Chên, earthquake, or movement within the earth. The meanings attributed to Tui and Chên are not the most common ones, but they are to be found in the reference material[20].

This would seem to establish good grounds for regarding the World of Thought as a vertical arrangement, making a contrasting pair with the World of the Senses. However, while on this subject, a few words might be said about the treatment of this arrangement by certain Western scholars who it would, perhaps, be impolite to name. Taking the arrangement as horizontal and cardinally oriented, they have a tendency to invert the diagram so that 'North' is at the top, presumably for the gratification of readers assumed to be unable to cope with the Chinese orientation. It should hardly be necessary to point out that in doing so they unwittingly perpetrate a farce, for they thus end up with Heaven below the ground and Earth in the sky.

If such a horizontal cardinal orientation has to be discarded, and especially the North-South axis, it is still possible, however, to retain an East-West orientation (so long as the arrangement is not inverted, of course). In this case Li, the sun, would represent the East, and K'an, the moon, would represent the West. Once the arrangement is regarded as vertical another meaning presents itself. This is that the arrangement displays the apparent motion of the sun during a 24 hour period; or to put it another way, as displaying the rise and fall of the yang and yin during a single day. This is shown in Figure 19.

Looking toward the South (the direction of the sun, and the most important direction in Chinese thinking), the sun moves in a clockwise direction. The sun is the primary embodiment of yang, and for our purposes here, we can take daylight as yang, nighttime as yin. Starting with Li in the East, we find that this is the first time in the clockwise motion of the circle where the yang lines

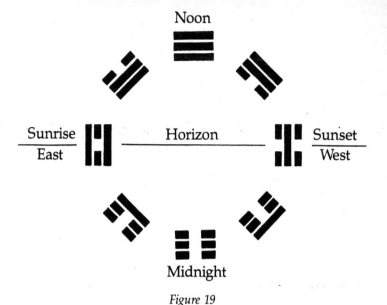

Noon

Sunrise
East

Horizon

Sunset
West

Midnight

Figure 19

outnumber the yin. This would then correspond with dawn. The sun then climbs into the sky, its heat and 'power' increasing, through Tui. It reaches its zenith at Ch'ien, noon, the most powerful manifestation of yang in the sequence. In the afternoon it starts to decline, and its power decreases, the yin entering the trigram Sun. Sunset is at K'an, in the West, where the yin lines outnumber the yang for the first time. The sun is then apparently under the ground and the darkness increases. The yin lines preponderate, ultimately so at K'un, midnight. In the pre-dawn, the yang re-enters the trigram Chên, and the sun reappears once more at Li.

This possibility of starting to read the sequence from the position of Li brings us to another interesting facet of the arrangement. It will be recalled that the usual system of numeration for this arrangement runs to and fro, first anti-clockwise, then clockwise, as in Figure 20.

Let us now see what happens when we apply another, similar numeration system to the arrangement. This order is still divided into two opposite halves, but it starts from Li rather than Ch'ien, and runs first clockwise, then anti-clockwise. The resulting pattern is shown in Figure 21.

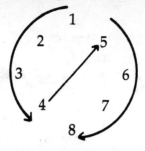

Figure 20

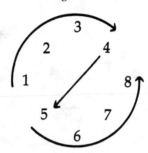

Figure 21

Figure 22

The Five Elements are not usually assigned to the trigrams in the World of Thought sequence, but if we do so, an extremely interesting picture emerges, as in Figure 22.

Reading round the arrangement in this order gives a representation of the Destruction cycle of the Five Elements:

Fire destroys Metal destroys Wood destroys Earth destroys Water
  (1)   (2,3)   (4,5)   (6,7)   (8)

With the Destruction cycle shown to be present in the World of Thought arrangement, its connection with the Ho T'u becomes more clearly understandable. We have a symmetrical pairing: the Ho T'u containing the Generation cycle, the trigrams the Destruction cycle. We can note the similarity to the pairing examined in the last chapter, where the Lo Shu contains the Destruction cycle, and the World of the Senses almost contains the Generation cycle. That arrangement was almost perfect, but not quite. However, such a Lo Shu/trigram, Destruction/Generation arrangement matching that of the Ho T'u/World of Thought can be found in the third arrangement of trigrams, to be examined in the next chapter.

As in the last chapter, let us conclude by summarizing a few points about the World of Thought arrangement. It shows the interchange of yang and yin as idealized cosmic principles. The Destruction cycle of the Five Elements. A vertical diagram of Heaven and Earth, as 'sky' and 'ground'. A 24-hour time progression illustrating the apparent motion of the sun. Slightly altered by the omission of K'an and Li, it shows a monthly time progression illustrating the phases of the moon. Finally, combined with the Ho T'u it makes a symmetrically paired arrangement; the trigrams showing the Destruction cycle of the Elements, the Ho T'u the Generation cycle.

6
The World of the Elements Arrangement

Having dealt with the two major circular arrangements of the trigrams, both of which have a considerable literature attached to them, we now come to the more obscure third sequence, about which very little has been recorded. It is, indeed, so obscure that it appears to have no name, and the term 'World of the Elements' is coined here for the first time to distinguish it from the other two sequences. The arrangement appears in Figure 23.

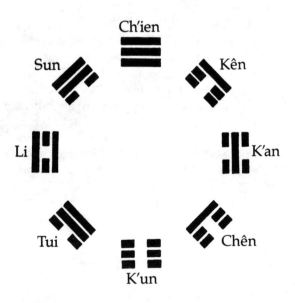

Figure 23

John Blofeld gives this sequence in the appendix to his translation of the *I Ching* under the title 'The Trigrams in the arrangement used in charms for warding off evil'[1]. He goes on to say: 'It is possible that this arrangement resulted from the ignorance of some fortune-teller at the popular level; there may well be a better reason for it, but it is not immediately apparent'. This would appear to be all that has been published in English about the arrangement.

Blofeld deserves our admiration for his frankness on the subject, and our thanks for rescuing this arrangement from obscurity. It is also possible to feel a great deal of sympathy with his bafflement. The makers of popular charms and talismans tend to be none too precise in their use of the trigrams, having a disconcerting habit of turning the arrangements inside out so that the bottom line of the trigram is on the outside of the circle. The manufacturers of geomantic compasses make a similar reversal. In this, however, they are by no means so bad as the Tibetans, who seem to have borrowed the trigrams from the Chinese with little comprehension of their meaning. Tibetan charms and astrological diagrams frequently use only six or seven of the trigrams, repeating one or two of them to make up the number eight, and then arranging them in a completely random sequence.

However, the World of the Elements sequence *does* contain a coherent logic, and it also has a slender history in the Chinese material on the *I Ching*. Before turning to this, let us see what can be inferred from the sequence at face value.

The arrangement shows considerable similarities to the World of Thought sequence. It too can be seen as a spirallic arrangement, but unlike the World of Thought, there seems to be no evidence of growth or decay here. It is simply a case of one yang line moving through a 'medium' of yin, at the right of the diagram; and of one yin line moving through a 'medium' of yang at the left. However, such a motion is the reverse of that shown in the World of Thought. There it is centrifugal, the yang ascending and moving out from the centre in a clockwise direction. Here it is centripetal, the yang descending and moving inwards in a clockwise direction.

This can also be seen as a vertical arrangement, with Heaven at the top and Earth at the bottom. The trigrams are arranged in the same pairs of complimentary opposites as the World of Thought. However, while the pairs Ch'ien/K'un and K'an/Li occupy the same positions as they do in the World of Thought, the pairs

Chên/Sun and Kên/Tui have switched positions with one another.

In this arrangement the majority of yang lines fall at the left of the diagram, while the majority of yin lines fall at the right. With the yang representing South and the yin North, it is possible to see this sequence as being a vertical arrangement on the North-South axis. By contrast, the World of Thought can be seen as a vertical arrangement on the East-West axis.

An interpretation of the structure of this sequence can be made along two completely separate lines: by the familial aspects of the trigrams, and by their Elements. Interestingly, there is no conflict between these interpretations; they are completely complimentary. We shall begin with the familial aspects.

These family attributes were mentioned in Chapter 1. There we saw that Ch'ien is the father, K'un the mother, Chên the eldest son, and so forth. In modern commentatory material on the *I Ching*, such familial aspects are usually connected with the World of the Senses arrangement. There appears to be no intrinsic reason for this connection, and it seems probable that the familial aspects and the World of the Senses originally had quite separate origins. In the World of the Senses the trigrams appear in two familial clusters. The female trigrams are arranged from the South-East (Sun) to the West (Tui); the male trigrams from the North-West (Ch'ien) to the East (Chên). They are not, however, in any logical or symmetrical order.

Nonetheless, the familial aspects of the trigrams are extremely important in the silk manuscript of the *I Ching* found at Ma-wang-tui. There they are used to order the arrangement of the hexagrams. Full details of this arrangement will be found in Appendix One. In the silk manuscript we find that the hexagrams are arranged in eight groups of eight, and that the eight hexagrams in a group all share the same upper trigram. These eight groups are then arranged by sex, as follows.

UPPER TRIGRAMS

1. Ch'ien	Father	5. K'un	Mother
2. Kên	3rd Son	6. Tui	3rd Daughter
3. K'an	2nd Son	7. Li	2nd Daughter
4. Chên	1st Son	8. Sun	1st Daughter

Exactly the same order of the trigrams will be found in the World of the Elements sequence, reading round clockwise from Ch'ien. It is tempting to suggest that the Ma-wang-tui manuscript represents a separate school of interpretation of the *I Ching*, which subsequently died out and disappeared from the literature. It would appear that only fragmentary ideas have survived from this school. One of these surviving ideas would seem to be the familial aspects of the trigrams, which have since been absorbed, without apparent logic or understanding, by the World of the Senses arrangement. Another survivor may be the World of the Elements arrangement of the trigrams. In the absence of any literature deriving from this school of interpretation, the meaning of the arrangement would, however, be lost. Similarly, the absence of such literature makes it impossible to be categorical about the date of the arrangement. Nonetheless, a Han dynasty origin is by no means inconceivable.

The arrangement reappears in the Sung dynasty, but once again under circumstances which suggest little or no understanding of its structure. Figure 24 features this arrangement, although the trigrams appear by name only, rather than as linear figures. The diagram comes from the *I Ching Chên Ch'üan*, [2] and appears under the title 'Ancient Lo Shu'. No particular significance should be attached to the word 'Ancient' here. Figure 15, reproduced in Chapter 5 and from the same source, also appears under the title of 'Ancient Ho T'u'. That, as we have seen, is probably a product of the same dynasty, the Sung.

The edition of the *I Ching Chên Ch'üan* used here is that of the *Sao Yeh Shan Fang* publishing house, and is dated 1869. It is printed from woodblocks, and claims to be a complete and unchanged reprint of a Sung dynasty edition. However, Figure 24 contains a number of obvious mistakes. It is, of course, uncertain whether these mistakes originated in the Sung dynasty edition or the nineteenth century reprint. It is possible that the nineteenth century block-cutter failed to understand the precise nature of the diagram he was reproducing. Be this as it may, a literal translation (including mistakes) appears in Figure 25. The mistaken captions are marked with an asterisk.

The numbers of the Lo Shu have been reproduced correctly with the exception of seven (middle right), which has been mistakenly replaced with the similar character for 'Earth'. Again, the Elements attached to the numbers three and eight are given as Water, rather than Wood. These characters are also similar to one another and it is quite obvious that we are dealing with simple mistakes here, rather than a variant form of the diagram.

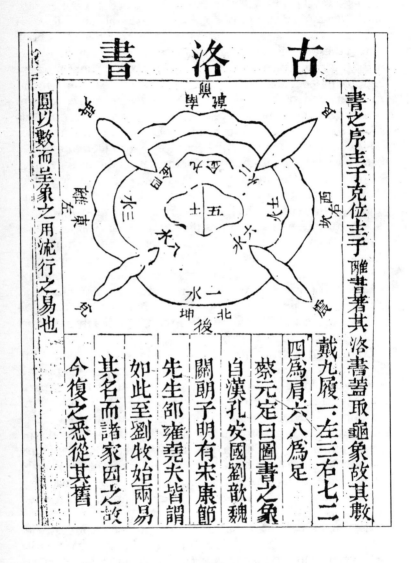

Figure 24

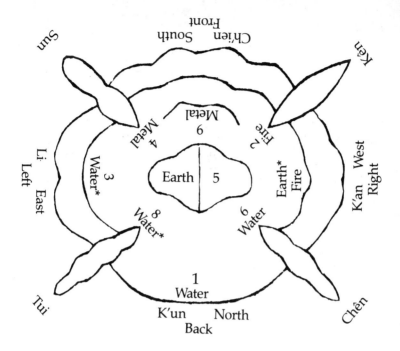

Figure 25

The accompanying text informs us that Figure 24 is a 'Tortoise Diagram', and assigns the numbers as follows: 'At the head is nine, leading back to one (at the tail). At the left is three, at right seven. Two and four are at the shoulders. Six and eight are at the (back) feet.' Looking at the actual linear figure it can be seen that, curiously shaped, it represents the tortoise itself, with a shell and four legs, although without a head or tail. More than this, however, the figure contains the numbers of the Lo Shu in its curved outlines. At the 'back' of the shell, one is represented by a single curve. The right front leg represents two, with two curves. The left side of the shell has three curves, and so forth. Five is represented by four curves and a straight line, while nine requires three separate sets of curves, of four, three and two respectively.

The accompanying text also quotes Ts'ai Yüan Ting (AD 1135–1198), who traces a lineage of *I Ching* scholars who preserved the diagram from the Han to the Sung dynasties, in chronological order. From the Han dynasty are mentioned K'ung An Kuo (156–74 BC) and Liu Hsin (c. 46 BC–AD 23). From the (Northern) Wei dynasty, Master Kuan Lang (fourth to fifth centuries AD) and Ming Yu (whose dates I have been unable to find). From the Sung, 'the great sage' Shao Yung (AD 1011–1077), whose courtesy name, Mister K'ang Chieh, is also given, and Liu Mu (AD 1011–1064). Even if such a lineage could be verified, it remains uncertain whether it refers to the arrangement of trigrams shown here, or simply to the transmission of the Lo Shu diagram. Of the numerical properties of the Lo Shu, or of the unusual arrangement of the trigrams, there is no mention whatsoever.

However, it is the numbers of the Lo Shu which give us the clue to the Elemental interpretation of this arrangement. Figure 26 shows the sequence of trigrams in relation to the magic square of three, with the normal Elemental attributes of the trigrams.

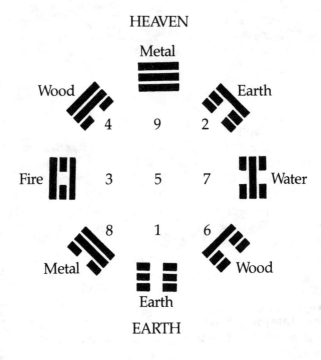

Figure 26

Let us now 'read' the sequence of the trigrams in the numerical order of the magic line of three, but in reverse, from nine (Heaven) to one (Earth). We discover that they are ordered according to the Generation cycle of the Five Elements, as follows:

Metal		9, 8	Ch'ien, Tui
	generates		
Water		7	K'an
	generates		
Wood		6, 4	Chên, Sun
	generates		
Fire		3	Li
	generates		
Earth		2, 1	Kên, K'un

The number five is, of course, omitted from this sequence, as it is the number of the centre and does not correspond with a trigram. There is a pleasing symmetry about this correlation of trigrams to Elements, with two trigrams to the first Element, one to the second, and so forth, giving a series that pivots round the centre of two, one, two, one, two.

In Chapter 5 it was shown that the passage from section three of the *Shuo Kua Chuan* was given a rather dubious connection with the World of the Thought arrangement. A similar forced interpretation of the same passage could also be applied to this arrangement. The trigrams are linked in the same pairs of complimentary opposites. 'That which is to come depends on the backward movement' could be interpreted as referring to the fertilizing influences of Heaven moving down to Earth through the Generation cycle, using 'backward moving numbers' from nine to one. 'That which is going into the past' could refer to the same influences returning to their source, using a 'forward movement' from one to nine. This thought is offered less in the hope of proving that the *Shuo Kua Chuan* refers to this arrangement, than in showing that almost *anything* can be read into the passage! Nonethless, the section of the *Shuo Kua Chuan* in question was found in association with the Ma-wang-tui manuscript and thus may derive from that school of interpretation; so perhaps the idea is not so preposterous after all.

We have seen that this arrangement can be interpreted in two completely different ways. The trigrams are arranged in a sequence which precisely reflects the familial order of the trigrams in the Ma-wang-tui manuscript; and they also show the Generation cycle of the Elements with reference to the magic square of three. If the Elements had been attributed to the individual trigrams before the formation of this sequence, the fact that the arrangement can be interpreted in two quite separate but complementary ways would be an extremely remarkable coincidence. There is another way of looking at the problem, however. This would suppose that the arrangement had first been drawn up to reflect the familial aspects of the trigrams. A second stage (although possibly contemporaneous with the first) would be to place the magic square of three on the arrangement and then to attribute the Elements to the trigrams from this, according to the Generation cycle. In essence, such a theory would argue that both the attribution of the Elements and the familial aspects to the trigrams originated with this particular sequence. This is perhaps a more logically acceptable explanation of the structure of the arrangement than that which supposes an astonishing coincidence between the two interpretations. Such an explanation would have serious consequences in terms of dating.

In Chapter 4 it was pointed out that the World of the Senses arrangement used the Elemental designations of the trigrams, although there was nothing in the literature attached to the arrangement to suggest why the Elements were attributed to particular trigrams. It appears that in the World of the Senses it was simply taken as an accepted fact that Tui (lake) corresponded with Metal, Chên (thunder) with Wood, and so forth. The impression to be drawn from this is that the Elemental designations of the trigrams existed before the World of the Senses. They would then have been drawn from another source and used in the construction of the Senses sequence to place the trigrams, by Element, in the cardinal directions, and to compose the mythical geography reflected in the arrangement. A similar state of affairs seems to exist with regard to the familial aspects of the trigrams. They are mentioned in association with the World of the Senses, but there is no systematic logic to their positioning in that arrangement. These aspects appear to have been drawn from another source as well. If the source of both these designations was the World of the Elements, it would suggest that this sequence was in fact the earliest of the three arrangements, having priority to both the Worlds of the Senses and of Thought. In effect, the World of the Elements would be the original arrangement of the trigrams.

One final point to be made concerns the symmetry that appears when the trigrams of this sequence are arranged round the Lo Shu. We have seen in Chapter 4 that the Lo Shu itself contains the Destruction cycle of the Elements in its numbering, while we now know that the trigrams of the World of the Elements arrangement contain the Generation cycle. A similar but reversed symmetry appeared with the World of Thought sequence and the Ho T'u, where the trigrams show the Destruction cycle and the Ho T'u the Generation cycle. It seems a reasonable assumption that the pairing of the World of Thought and the Ho T'u was drawn up to provide a match with the pairing of the World of the Elements and the Lo Shu. When the World of the Elements dropped out of use, the Lo Shu would then presumably have been attached to the World of the Senses, where it does not fit anywhere near as well. What is perhaps the most surprising fact is that the World of the Elements arrangement, and the associated Ma-wang-tui school of interpretation, should have been so entirely neglected. Despite its great intrinsic interest, it seems to have almost completely disappeared from view some 2000 years ago.

Our summary of this arrangement is necessarily brief. No time progression is immediately apparent. The arrangement appears to be vertical, and probably aligned on a North-South axis. It shows the familial relationships of the trigrams in a much more coherent form than either of the other two sequences. It shows the Generation cycle of the Five Elements and may, indeed, provide the origin for their attribution to the individual trigrams. Lastly, when shown in conjunction with the Lo Shu, it provides a symmetrical arrangement of the Generation and Destruction cycles of the Elements.

7

The Three Worlds As One

It should by now have become apparent that the Han dynasty cosmological system was infinitely more flexible and complex than it first appeared. Certain of the interpretations offered in previous chapters have been unconventional, but hardly out of context with Han thought. This chapter is more speculative and continues the same unconventional line of thought. However, it contains nothing beyond the capabilities of the Han philosophers.

It has been shown that the entire correlative system, including the trigrams, Elements and 'magic' numbers, was integrated into a single all-encompassing system, and that this was used to provide a number of microcosmic models. Such microcosms were used to interpret the universe and, by their use in religious and magic rituals, to gain control over it, or at least to ensure the continuance of its normal function.

However, the three microcosmic arrangements of trigrams that have been discussed so far have all been 'one-dimensional', existing in only a single plane, whether it be horizontal or vertical. The following pages will show how these three sequences of trigrams can be integrated into a symbolic model of the universe in three dimensions. As one of these sequences does not appear at all in the surviving commentatory material, it is obviously impossible to find a historical forerunner for such a three-dimensional model. However, the model to be discussed here is that of the universe as it would have been perceived in the Han dynasty, described in traditional terms. While it might be possible and tempting to draw analogies between, for instance, the spiral nature of the Ho T'u numbers and the spiral nature of the galaxy, such analogies would be outside our terms of reference. We are here dealing with a geocentric view of the universe, in which the earth is flat, central, and does not move.

This flat Earth provides the first stage of the model, the outer edges of which are represented by the World of the Senses arrangement. This is shown horizontal and oriented toward the four cardinal points, as in Figure 27. China itself, or 'the whole of the known world', would be represented by the nine provinces of the Lo Shu, within the circle of the trigrams; but for the sake of simplicity this is omitted from the diagram.

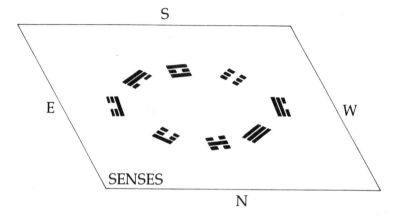

Figure 27

We can now integrate the two vertical sequences of trigrams with this, starting with the World of the Elements arrangement, which it has been suggested lies along the North-South axis. As will be seen from Figure 28, the two sequences interlock through the equivalent positions in each of Li in the South and K'an in the North. It will be recalled that in the World of the Elements those trigrams with the majority of yang lines cluster round Li and fall on the southern side of the diagram, which is the yang direction. Similarly, the trigrams with the majority of yin lines cluster round K'an and fall toward the North, the yin direction. Ch'ien, Heaven, is at the zenith, while K'un, Earth, is at the nadir.

The final stage is to add the World of Thought arrangement, which lies along the East-West axis, as in Figure 29. This sequence interlocks with that of the Elements through the equivalent position

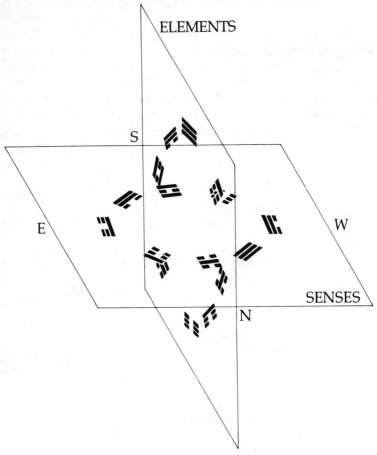

Figure 28

in each of the trigrams Ch'ien at the zenith and K'un at the nadir.

Apparently more difficult to explain is the way in which Li (of the World of Thought) interlocks with Chên (of the World of the Senses), and K'an (Thought) with Tui (Senses). For this we must recall the mythological explanation of the World of the Senses arrangement offered in Chapter 4. There it was shown that the sun rises from the Fu Sang tree on the island of P'êng Lai. Here the sun is represented by the trigram Li in the World of Thought. P'êng Lai is represented by Chên in the World of the Senses, and

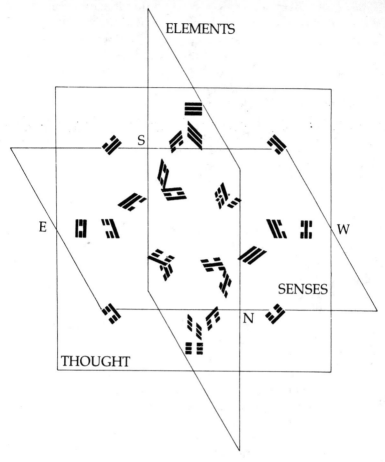

Figure 29

the Element of this trigram is Wood, representing the Fu Sang tree. Li and Chên thus interlock. A similar connection was pointed out between the moon (represented by K'an in the World of Thought) and Yü Yüan, the lake in the K'un Lun mountains (represented by Tui in the World of the Senses). This pair of trigrams therefore interlock in the same way as Li and Chên.

A similar way of looking at this connection would be to recall that the World of Thought arrangement shows the path of the sun during a 24 hour period. It rises from P'êng Lai, represented by

Chên in the World of the Senses, then travels across the sky. Its course is shown by the World of Thought sequence, and then it plunges into Yü Yüan, represented by Tui in the World of the Senses.

It is also possible to see here the great bird Hsi Yu, 'Seldom Seen', represented by the cruciform arrangement of trigrams that lie above the World of the Senses sequence. Hsi Yu is said to face South, stretching his left wing to cover Tung Wang Kung, his right to cover Hsi Wang Mu. Once each year, Hsi Wang Mu climbs upon his wing, crosses over his back, and visits her consort[1]. Hsi Yu's body would be represented by the trigrams Sun (head), Ch'ien and Kên (tail) in the Elements sequence. His wings would be represented in the World of Thought sequence, the left wing by Li and Tui, the right by Sun and K'an.

A more obvious correlation can be found between this three-dimensional trigram model and an independent cosmological system which may date as early as the third century BC, and which was certainly current in the Han dynasty. We have seen that the sky was thought to be supported by either four or eight columns, represented by mountains. Of these columns, the four major ones were correlated with the cardinal points. These four columns were thought to be connected by a pair of 'ropes', *shêng* or *wei*. More particularly, these are thought of as the same type of ropes as those used in a Han dynasty chariot. This concept is taken from the *Kai-T'ien* school of cosmology, which likened the Earth to the square body of the chariot, and Heaven to the round umbrella or canopy mounted above it. These 'ropes' were arranged in a cross between the four columns, North-South and East-West, and supported the sky[2]. It is possible to see these 'ropes' represented by the cruciform arrangement of the trigrams that appear above the World of the Senses, composed of those same parts of the Worlds of Thought and Elements mentioned in relation to Hsi Yu. Furthermore, these 'ropes' arise from the plane of the World of the Senses at Chên, Li, Tui and K'an. As was pointed out in the *I Wei*, these were known as *Chêng*, or 'uprights', and correspond by their positions to the numbers in the Lo Shu which represent four of the cardinal mountains.

Beyond these mythical connotations, our symbolic representation of the universe now includes the following:
The world in three planes: horizontal, vertical North-South and vertical East-West.

The surface of the Earth (World of the Senses) with the heavens above (the two trigrams Ch'ien) and the body of the Earth below (the two trigrams K'un).

A number of time progressions: the daily movement of the sun and the monthly phases of the moon (World of Thought); the annual progression of the seasons and the natural life-cycle from birth to death (World of the Senses).

The Generation cycle of the Five Elements (World of the Elements) and the Destruction cycle of the same (World of Thought).

The interchange of yang and yin as cosmic principles (World of Thought).

This presents a beautifully complete model containing all the major elements of the Han world-view: the yang and yin, the Five Elements, time, astronomy, geography, numerology, cosmology and mythology. Furthermore, if the interpretations of the individual trigram arrangements are thought to be somewhat revolutionary, those interpretations would appear to be strengthened by the fact that in this, the final model, they slot together so neatly.

Part Three
Masters of the Mysterious

8
The Devil Valley Diagram

Having so far concentrated almost entirely on the internal structure of the various trigram sequences, in this final section our attention will turn to their broader application. A discussion of the use of the trigrams on the battlefield and in Taoist ritual magic will follow in the next chapter. Here we will examine a complex six-level diagram which integrates the trigrams with a number of other aspects of the correlative cosmology already discussed.

The diagram itself is shown in Figure 30. It is difficult to date, although internal evidence to be discussed below suggests that the form in which it now exists originated several hundred years after the Han dynasty. However, the origin of its various components can be dated to the Han, the major period of correlative thought, and it is by no means inconceivable that some primeval form of the diagram dates from the same period. Lack of information prevents the reaching of a definite conclusion. Although the Han cosmology ceased to be of philosophical interest shortly after the fall of that dynasty, it must be recalled that on a more popular level the process of correlation continued for centuries, reaching its final culmination in the enormously complex geomancer's compasses of the Ming and Ch'ing dynasties.

The magnetic compass itself is closely connected to our subject, its earliest form being conjecturally connected to the Diviner's Boards of the Han dynasty. These boards, whose precise usage is no longer understood, consisted of two plates, one square, the other round. The square plate represented the Earth and was marked with symbols including the Celestial Stems, the Terrestrial Branches and the 28 constellations or Lunar Mansions. Mounted on top of this and pivoted at the centre was the round Heaven plate.

This was marked with similar symbols and usually also displayed the seven stars of the Plough. Known to the Chinese as the Dipper, this was the most important of the constellations in ritual and religion, having connections with the axis of the world and the Polar Palace of Heaven. The compass itself appears to have developed by replacing the round Heaven plate with a ladle-shaped pointer made of loadstone, the shape of which suggests that it actually represented the Dipper. This carefully balanced and polished pointer rotated at the centre of the square Earth plate. The development of this primitive compass appears to date at least as early as the second century AD, if not before[1].

In the present state of our knowledge, it is uncertain whether these early Diviner's Boards and compasses had any connection with 'geomancy'. This, the most common Western term for the Chinese words *Fêng Shui*, hardly does the system justice. 'Geomancy' literally means only 'divination from the earth'. *Fêng Shui*, literally 'wind and water', concerns itself with deducing *all* the celestial and terrestrial influences relative to a certain locality, with the intention of finding the most auspicious sites for house-building, grave-making, or simply improving the fortunes of the inhabitants. The practitioner is required to have a knowledge of astrology, directionology relative to both true and magnetic North, the Five Elements, the trigrams, the prevailing winds and the flow of water, as well as making his judgements according to the morphology of the terrestrial features. The system's most primeval form can be traced back to the fourth and third centuries BC, although it was only consolidated in the Later Han dynasty and the succeeding Three Kingdoms Period[2]. Most of the literature on the subject is far later, and the majority of it dates from the last thousand years. The *Fêng Shui* system represents the major survival of the correlative cosmology that developed in the Han dynasty. However, like the *I Ching* itself, it is not a product of 'ancient wisdom' dating from prehistoric times; rather it has evolved through a process of slow development over a number of centuries.

The widespread availability of the magnetic compass is a relatively recent development, and its association with the *Fêng Shui* system dates from the Ming and Ch'ing dynasties. The beautiful geomancer's instruments of the Ch'ing have a dial of up to 24 circular divisions containing virtually all the elements of the correlative cosmology. Included are the trigrams (both major arrangements), the hexagrams, the Celestial Stems, the Terrestrial Branches, the Five Elements, the 28 constellations, the degrees of the circle (both the ancient system which divided the horizon into 365¼ degrees to match the days of the year, and the imported Western system of 360 degrees), and many others. The *Fêng Shui* system and its compasses have been described in detail elsewhere, most notably by Feuchtwang[3]. As it is a much later development in which the trigrams play only a minor part, we must pass over the subject briefly here.

However, during the approximately 1500 years between the inception of the correlative system and its culmination in the compasses of the Ming and Ch'ing, there must have been various intermediate stages. The diagram shown in Figure 30 may well represent just such a stage.

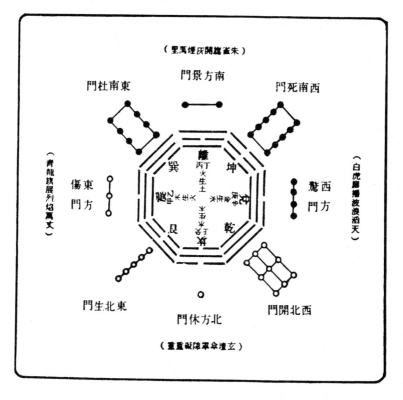

Figure 30

The name 'Devil Valley Diagram' is once again a label of convenience and may have to be discarded if new information appears. As with the World of the Elements arrangement of the trigrams, there appears to be no literature relating to this diagram in the English language.

The diagram appears on the front cover of a series of books published in Hong Kong purporting to expound the teachings of Kuei Ku Tzŭ, 'The Master of Devil Valley'. These books have titles such as *Kuei Ku Tzŭ's Secret Book of Heaven*, on Chinese astrology and astral magic; *Kuei Ku Tzŭ's Divine Occult Strategy*, on esoteric military matters; *Kuei Ku Tzŭ's Thirty-six Matchless Spirit Invocations*, and so forth[4]. All are written by a certain Ch'ên Ying Lüeh, and are undated, although the editions in my possession were purchased in the 1970s. All of them, regardless of subject matter, have this diagram as the cover illustration. However, there appears to be no direct connection between the diagram and the text of the works themselves, and no reference appears to it anywhere.

These books are certainly modern productions and seem to have little connection with the original figure of Kuei Ku Tzŭ. The nearest equivalent in the Western world would seem to be, say, a modern compendium of fortune-telling methods given a title such as 'Merlin's Book of Prophetic Arts'. The attribution of recent material to ancient worthies who doubtless never had anything to do with the subject is a well-established tradition in China. As has been noted with Fu Hsi and King Wên, the practice can be traced back at least 2000 years. It may also give the reader pause to reflect on the fact that the purely philosophical speculations of the Han dynasty should now have ended up in the form of 'magic diagrams' on the covers of a cheap line of paperbacks.

That there was a real person who assumed the name of the Master of Devil Valley (in Chinese, Kuei Ku) appears to be fairly well established. That said, all else becomes rather confused. The historical figure is dated to the fourth century BC; although how much or how little of the surviving *Kuei Ku Tzŭ* book, dating from the same period, should be attributed to him is less certain. It contains a mixture of Taoist and Legalist philosophy, and seems to have had nothing whatsoever to do with divination or magic[5].

Moving into the domain of legend, we find that one candidate for the Master's title is a certain Wang Hsü, who lived at Kuei Ku.

However, *which* Kuei Ku is uncertain, as there are at least four places in China having this name. Wang is said to have been a master of yin-yang theory, applying it to both political and military affairs. This connection with military matters is interesting, as we shall discover certain military aspects attached to the diagram under discussion. Wang Hsü is said to have been the teacher of two famous and well-authenticated political figures of the Warring States period, Su Chin and Chang Yi[6].

Wang Hsü's career is also dated to the sixth century BC, however; an inconsistency which is 'explained' in terms of his having reincarnated several times. Here, of course, we are dealing with purely mythic and much later traditions. This material places his first appearance in the world in the time of the primeval Yellow Emperor, under whom he is said to have studied natural history, medicinal plants and the fluctuations of the yang and yin. At a later date he became an immortal and especially skilled in divination, with which his name has become synonymous in modern times. He was also deified in recent centuries as the God of Spectacle Sellers. This position was given to him because most diviners in traditional China were blind or half-blind, and thus in need of spectacles[7]!

One last folk-tale is worthy of attention before moving on to more serious matters. It refers to a cave in Kiangsi province, and the events narrated are said to have occurred in the Han dynasty. The story centres round a certain poor herdsman called Chang, whose only surviving relative was his grandmother. One day, while near the cave, he heard someone saying: 'Stone-door open; Mister Kuei Ku is coming!' The door of the cave opened and the newcomer entered, leaving again later with a similar command which closed the door after him. Having learned the phrase, Chang entered the cave at an opportune moment, but found nothing within. Returning home he told his grandmother about the cave, and she expressed a desire to see it. However, when he took her there she became lost. Chang, assuming that she had gone home before him, left the cave. Failing to find her outside, he tried to regain entry, only to find that the magic phrase no longer worked. On the return of Kuei Ku Tzŭ, Chang implored him to open the cave, but the Master refused. He explained that the grandmother's disappearance was a matter of fate, and that the cave demanded a victim. Had the victim been male, every generation of Chang's posterity would have been a prince; being female, the descendants would possess power over demons. Chang returned home, married, and produced a son. This was Chang Ling, later to be known as Chang Tao Ling, the first of the Taoist 'Heavenly Masters' (sometimes known in the West as 'Taoist Popes'), and traditionally the founder of the popular Taoist religion. The sect of the Heavenly Masters is specially known for its rites of exorcism. It might also be noted that it was the Taoist religion which did much to preserve the correlative and divinatory systems of the Han in later times[8].

After this lengthy preamble, the time has come to return to the diagram, an English translation of which is given in Figure 31. It is composed of six concentric rings, and one is tempted to compare this structure with the six line positions of an *I Ching* hexagram.

The Red Bird banner reveals ashes, smoking for 10,000 *li*

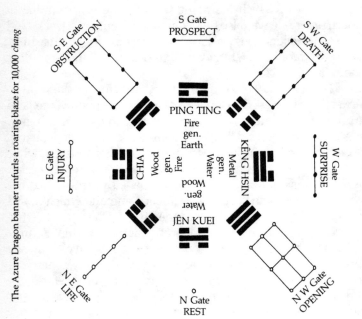

The Dark Terrace parasol extends a strong barricade

Figure 31

To this we will return shortly, after an examination of the individual rings. In common with the geomancer's compass, of which this ring-system may possibly be an early forerunner, the structure will be treated from the centre outwards. Thus the innermost ring is here numbered one, the outermost six.

Rings One and Six

These two rings are treated together, as both refer to the Generation cycle of the Five Elements.

Ring One. Here, in the simple form of a three-character phrase, are four of the five stages of the Generation cycle: 'Wood generates Fire', 'Fire generates Earth', and so forth. The first word in each phrase is correlated with the direction appropriate to it, and gives rise to the Element of the next direction, reading clockwise. Thus Wood, in the East, gives rise to Fire. Fire in the South gives rise to Earth. Earth, however, being the Element of the Centre, is omitted from the diagram, and the next stage begins with its product, Metal. This, in the West, gives rise to Water, and Water in the North gives rise to Wood. This obviously represents the Generation cycle in its most basic and straightforward form.

Ring Six. In this 'ring' (shown square in the diagram, presumably merely as a product of printing the wording in straight lines), the same cycle is repeated. Here, however, the Generation cycle appears in a much more mythical and poetic form, each sentence consisting of exactly eight characters in Chinese.

The first hint of a military application also appears here. The use of flags and banners correlated with the Five Elements and the directions is at least as old as the Han dynasty. Such matters are mentioned in the *Li Chi* (the 'Book of Rites') which allegedly deals with the rites and ceremonies of the Chou dynasty, but which was probably compiled in the Earlier Han. With reference to the army, it says: 'On the march the banner with the Red Bird should be in front; that with the Dark Warrior behind; that with the Azure Dragon on the left; and that with the White Tiger on the right'. A similar passage can be found in the military manual attributed to Wu Ch'i, who lived in the fourth century BC, although the book itself is undoubtedly a later compilation[9]. The army being taken as marching South, these banners correlate with the appropriate directions, and match the phrases used in the diagram.

Starting in the East, Ring Six has '*The Azure Dragon banner unfurls a roaring blaze for 10,000 chang*'. The Azure Dragon is the symbolic animal of the East, and of the Element Wood. It produces a roaring blaze (Wood giving rise to Fire, as in Ring One) which stretches for 10,000 *chang*. A *chang* is a measure equivalent to 10 Chinese feet. Measurements have varied in different periods and locales, but in Han times the standard foot (*chih*) was about 9.1 English inches. One *chang* would thus measure seven feet seven inches in modern terms, and ten thousand would be equivalent to approximately fourteen and a third miles. However, the number ten thousand is also used for a 'myriad', or an indeterminably large number, so this could be taken to mean simply 'a great distance'.

In the South, shown as usual at the top of the diagram, there is: '*The Red Bird banner reveals ashes, smoking for 10,000 li*'. The Red Bird is the symbolic animal of the South, and of Fire. Fire gives rise to Earth, in the form of ashes, so once more there is a correspondence to the simple version in Ring One. A *li* is equivalent to 150 *chang* which, again using Han measurements, would be about 380 English yards. Ten thousand *li* would thus be equivalent to some 2,150 miles. Again, this might simply mean 'a great distance', although obviously there is a greater order of magnitude involved here than in the first phrase. It is possible that the inventor of the chart merely wished to avoid repeating the same distance as in the previous phrase. An alternative reason for this 150-fold increase might be that the South was considered the most important direction, that of the yang. In terms of an army on the march, it might also be considered auspicious to have this increase in importance attached to the front of the array, in the direction toward which it was intended to march. As is to be expected, the Element Earth, being connected with the Centre, is omitted.

The Western phrase reads: '*The White Tiger streamer scatters billowing waves, dashing to the sky*'. The White Tiger is the animal of the West, and of the Element Metal, which would have been produced by Earth, had that not been omitted. Metal gives rise to Water, here depicted in the form of billowing waves. The sea being to some extent 'immeasurable', the vast quantity is not shown in terms of distance, but rather in power: the waves 'dash to the sky'.

In the North is a phrase which at first sight seems slightly more difficult to interpret, though it still fits in with the general scheme: '*The Dark Terrace parasol extends a strong barricade*'. With the title

'Dark Terrace' we find ourselves in the realm of Chinese eclectic-
ism. Simply put, Dark Terrace (Hsüan T'an) is an alternative
name for Hsüan Wu, the Dark Warrior, the god and symbolic
representative of the North. However, this is also an abbreviation
for Hsüan T'an P'u-sa, the Boddhisattva of the Dark Terrace, or
Hsüan Yüan T'an P'u-sa, the Boddhisattva of the Primordial Dark
Terrace. P'u-sa, the Chinese transliteration of Boddhisattva, is
obviously a Buddhist term, but the title as a whole is of Moham-
medan origin. All this may seem unimportant, but the use of this
phrase does give some idea of the date of the diagram in its present
form: not before the eighth century AD, when Islam was first
introduced into China[10].

Naturally this only refers to our printed version of this diagram;
in essence, it could have been in existence before this, with a variant
name for the deity of the North. The mention of a parasol rather
than a flag or banner may seem curious, but the connection of
this item of regalia with military affairs is well attested from early
times. The chariots of the Han dynasty were frequently surmounted
by a parasol or umbrella, and the chariot is the natural transport
of a general[11]. It is thus an appropriate attribute of the Dark
Warrior, who also represents the Element Water. Water gives rise
to Wood, of which the extensive barricade backing up the rear of
the army is made, and so the cycle is completed.

It can thus be seen that Ring Six gives the Elemental Generation
cycle on a much more vast and elaborate scale than Ring One.
Not only are there military overtones, but the scale may even extend
to cosmic proportions. The four symbolic animals or rulers are also
used to denote the four quadrants of the heavens, each one being
given authority over seven of the 28 constellations.

Ring Two

Here are displayed eight of the Ten Celestial Stems, arranged
according to their Elemental and directional designations. As may
be expected, those referring to the Centre are omitted, in common
with the central omissions in Rings One and Six.

Apart from their use in pairs to indicate the directions, each of
the individual Stems is also said to have an 'affinity' to a particular
form of its Element. The first Stem of the pair is connected to the
Element in a primordial form, the second to a refined form[12].

The first and second Stems are *Chia* and *I*, with the directional bearing East and the Element Wood. *Chia's* affinity is with trees, *I's* with hewn timber. Third and fourth are *Ping* and *Ting*, correlated to South and Fire. *Ping* is connected to lightning, *Ting* to burning incense. *Wu* and *Chi*, fifth and sixth, are omitted, although it might be nearer to the inventor's intentions to say that they are 'taken as read'. They represent the Centre and Earth. Their affinities are to hills and earthenware respectively. Seventh and eighth are *Kêng* and *Hsin*, representing the West and Metal. These are connected respectively to metal ore and kettles. In the North lie *Jên* and *Kuei*, ninth and tenth, representing Water. Their affinities are to salt and fresh water respectively. Here then, under the guise of the Celestial Stems, are the same directional and Elemental correlates as in Rings One and Six. Once again, the Generation cycle is represented in a clockwise direction, with the omission of the Earth Element.

Ring Three

Here lie the eight trigrams in the World of the Senses arrangement, which has been fully dealt with in Chapter 4. Linked to each trigram is the Chinese character denoting its name, and these have been omitted in the English translation. However, it should be noted that the original Chinese diagram is misprinted. The linear figure of Tui is printed twice, in its own position and that of Chên. In the Chinese text, though, Chên is named correctly, and the mistake has been corrected in the English translation shown in Figure 31.

It will be recalled that the World of the Senses comes very close to representing the Generation cycle of the Elements. However, in view of the fact that the Generation cycle appears as a repeated motif in the other rings of this diagram, it might be expected that the World of the Elements arrangement would be more appropriate here than that of the Senses. That it is not used may be seen as further evidence of the neglect into which the World of the Elements had fallen. Doubtless the World of the Senses was felt to be so well-known and appropriate that it was thought to be adequate, in spite of its imperfections. As will become apparent, the Fourth and Fifth Rings are also correlated to the World of the Senses sequence even though, in the case of Ring Four, the Elements would provide a more neat and logical correlation. This suggests once again that the Elements sequence was unknown to the creator of the diagram.

It may also be noted once again that the four trigrams at the cardinal points of the Senses sequence correspond by Element with the two inner rings. Chên in the East has the Element Wood; Li in the South, Fire; Tui in the West, Metal; K'an in the North, Water.

Ring Four

This ring contains the numbers one to five and eight to 10. They are represented as patterns of dots similar to, but not identical with, the patterns used in the Ho T'u and Lo Shu diagrams. Odd numbers are represented by the white (yang) dots, even numbers by black (yin) dots.

These numbers are correlated by position to the World of the Senses trigrams shown in Ring Three, using a system of numbers, Elements and sex. In Chapter 4 the system of attributing the Elements to the numbers was discussed, which derived from the *Ta Chuan* and the *Shu Ching*. This, it will be recalled, gave a sequence beginning 'First, Heaven engendered Water; second, Earth engendered Fire,' and so forth. Added to this, Heaven is to be taken as male, Earth as female. There is thus an Element and sex for each number, and these are then correlated by position with the Element and sex of the trigrams in the World of the Senses arrangement. The complete sequence is as follows.

One: 'First, Heaven engendered Water'. One is thus a male, heavenly, odd number, correlated with Water. It is positioned to match K'an, a male trigram (the middle son), the Element of which is Water.

Two: 'Second, Earth engendered Fire'. Two is a female, earthly, even number, related to Fire. It is correlated with Li, a female trigram (the middle daughter), the Element of which is Fire.

Three: 'Third, Heaven engendered Wood'. Three is a male, heavenly, odd number, Element Wood. It is related to Chên, the eldest son, Element Wood.

Four: 'Fourth, Earth engendered Metal'. Four is a female, earthly, even number, Element Metal. It is linked with Tui, the youngest daughter, Element Metal.

Five: 'Fifth, Heaven engendered Earth'. Five is a male, heavenly, odd number, Element Earth. It is connected to Kên, the youngest son, Element Earth.

Eight: 'Eighth, Earth completed Wood'. Eight is a female, earthly, even number, Element Wood. It is correlated with Sun, the eldest daughter, Element Wood.

Nine: 'Ninth, Heaven completed Metal'. Nine is a male, heavenly, odd number, Element Metal. It is related to Ch'ien, the father, Element Metal.

Ten: 'Tenth, Earth completed Earth'. Ten is a female, earthly, even number, Element Earth. It is linked with K'un, the mother, Element Earth.

As is often the case, there is here a problem of correlation in that there are 10 numbers in the Elemental series and only eight trigrams. Water and Fire are connected with only one trigram each, while there are four numbers related to these two Elements. A choice obviously has to be made between retaining one and two, or six and seven. As the overriding theme of this diagram appears to be that of generation, one and two are retained, these being the numbers by which Water and Fire are engendered. Six and seven being the numbers by which they are completed thus become the obvious candidates for omission. Again, purely aesthetic considerations may be at work. It is more symmetrical to have the series of 10 numbers starting with one and two, and thus matching with the final numbers nine and 10, than to start the series from three and then run it straight through to the end.

A further reason for retaining these numbers in preference to the others is that when all the odd numbers are added up they give a total of 18, the even numbers of 24. When these totals are reduced to a single figure by adding the digits together, the odd, yang numbers result in nine, the number of the moving yang lines in the *I Ching*; the even numbers result in six, the number of the moving yin.

It is also to be noted that the numbers one to four lie at the cardinal points. Their Elemental designations also correlate with the directions, thus: one, Water, North; two, Fire, South; three, Wood, East; four, Metal, West. This brings this ring into line with the same correlative system found in rings one, two, three and six.

Ring Five

The fifth ring is more mysterious. Here is a series of eight gates, linked to the directions. These gates lie at the heart of the material to be discussed in the next chapter, and fuller details of them will be given there. They form the basis of the *Pa Chên*, the Eight Arrays, a mysterious battle-strategy based on the eight trigrams. It will be shown that these gates are correlated with the trigrams in the World of the Senses arrangement. They are also used in the *Ch'i-mên Tun-chia*, the Mysterious Gates of the Hidden Stems. This has two aspects. It is a complex divination system using a number of the elements in the correlative cosmology to define unlucky days and directions, according to the calendar based on the sexagenary cycle. It is also used in Taoist ritual magic.

Further discussion will have to be postponed until the next chapter, as the material takes us into areas far removed from the diagram at hand. For our present purposes, it is sufficient to say that the gates denote the World of the Senses trigrams in an amplified form; a form which includes a divination system, ritual magic and military strategy.

Overall Structure

The diagram consists of six concentric rings, and this number suggests another approach to its interpretation. This is by comparison with the internal structure of an *I Ching* hexagram. Of particular interest here is the way in which the trinity of Heaven, Earth and Man is represented in the trigrams and hexagrams.

In a trigram, the first (lowest) line is said to correspond to Earth, the second to Man, the third to Heaven. Similarly, in a hexagram the lowest two lines correspond to Earth, the third and fourth to Man, the fifth and sixth to Heaven.

The first and sixth lines of a hexagram are said to be 'outside the action'. The first line shows the situation before events unfold, the sixth the situation after their completion. In this diagram the Generation cycle lies in Rings One and Six, 'framing' the arrangement and present at its beginning and end. The simple version of the cycle lies in the Earth position, in terms of both trigram and hexagram correspondence. It thus provides a solid 'foundation' for the rest of the diagram.

The second line of a trigram is associated with Man. In the Second Ring of the diagram lie the Celestial Stems. These may be seen as an artificial creation, an invention of man, as opposed to the eternal Elementary cycle. The Celestial Stems correlate with the directions on the Earth. By one of those curious inversions which by now should seem commonplace, the Terrestrial Branches are used to designate time, or the movement of the celestial bodies. It should be pointed out that the Branches are also used to designate directions, but in nowhere near as satisfactory a manner; their main correlate is with the hours of the day and the months of the year.

In the correspondences of the hexagram, the second position is still correlated with Earth. The Celestial Stems thus fit neatly into the Second Ring. They are an invention of Man, used for defining the directions of the Earth. The second line of a hexagram is also said to correspond to the position of a country official, the 'man on the ground' as opposed to the rulers in the palace. It would be appropriate for such an official to have local geographical knowledge, here represented by the directional system of the Celestial Stems.

The third line of a trigram is a Heaven position, and in a hexagram it is the first to correspond with Man. In Chapter 4 it was shown that the World of the Senses sequence, with its mythic overtones, provided a link between the worlds of Man and Heaven. The third line of a hexagram also represents a place of transition, where the lower trigram meets the upper. There is no better symbol of transition and mutation than the eight trigrams.

The fourth line is an Earth trigram position, a Man hexagram position. A more mundane symbol might thus be expected, here provided by the numbers. These are shown in linear and rectangular shapes reminiscent of the markings of the Earth in the Lo Shu. They also have a human aspect in that they are divided by sex depending on whether they are odd or even, and they also correspond to the familial designations of the trigrams. The fourth line of the hexagram is said to correspond to that of a minister who assists the ruler in the fifth place. A knowledge of mathematics, and of human relationships, could doubtless be seen as assets to such a minister.

The Fifth Ring is the position of a king or ruler. A heavenly ruler at that, for while the trigram position is that of Man, the hexagram position is the first line of Heaven. One might call such a ruler 'The Superior Man'. This ring is connected with the trigrams, and also with magic and war; the latter two surely being the concerns of a heavenly ruler. It is also connected with an advanced divination system which concerns itself with both the directions and time. The Terrestrial Branches play a large part in the *Ch'i-mên Tun-chia* system, thus providing a symmetrical link with the use of the Celestial Stems in the Second Ring.

The sixth line occupies a Heavenly position in both trigram and hexagram. Here the Generation cycle is present once more, but on a cosmic scale, the symbolic animals being related to the constellations. There are also military applications linking it with the ruler in the fifth place. However, the sixth line is once again 'outside the action', matching with the first line. Here though it is on a much more exalted scale, and frames the entire sequence.

Overall, three basic areas of concern may be summarized. First is that of Earth, represented by the first two rings, where the two most important themes of the diagram first appear. These are the Generation cycle of the Five Elements and the directions, particularly the cardinal points. They are here represented in simple form. The second area is that of Man, represented by the Third and Fourth Rings. The themes here are change (the trigrams) and mathematics. Remembering the geographical connections of the World of the Senses sequence, this area could also be seen as an activity of man: measuring the Earth and imposing order on the world by number. The third area is that of Heaven, or the heavenly ruler, represented by the Fifth and Sixth Rings. Here the royal activity of warfare is reflected in both rings. Also present are magic, divination and, with the outer ring, astrology.

These speculations could probably be extended indefinitely. Such is the inherent nature of cosmic diagrams like the one presented here. While the military and directional aspects of the diagram are undoubtedly important, the overriding theme would seem to be the Generation cycle of the Five Elements which appears, if only indirectly, in at least five of the rings. However, with the military connotations of Rings Five and Six, it is quite possible that the Generation aspect reflects more a case of 'accentuating the positive' than that the diagram has any fertility associations. It may well be a magical talisman designed to promote success in war, or even an overly complicated magical extension of the Eight Arrays tactical system. It is to this last aspect that our attention will turn next.

9
The Eight Arrays

'A leader of an army should be able to go and come, to be facile and obdurate, to advance and retire, to show himself weak or strong, to be immovable as mountains, to be inscrutable as the operations of nature, to be infinite as the universe, to be everlasting as the blue void, to be vast as the ocean, to be dazzling as the lights of heaven, to foresee droughts and floods, to know the nature of the ground, to understand the possibilities of battle arrays, to conjecture the excellences and defects of the enemy.'

Attributed to Chu-ko Liang
Romance of the Three Kingdoms, Chapter 100[1].

At first sight it may seem an improbable if not impossible task to transfer the eight trigrams from the realms of philosophy and cosmology to the hard physical world of the battlefield. That such a transfer was thought to have been achieved is a matter of record, however, even if the details of the process remain unclear. It should be said at the outset that this chapter has no certain solutions to offer to the problems it raises. History has left a mystery which it may not be possible to solve after this lapse of time, although such a mystery can still be described and examined. If nothing else, it seems worthwhile assembling such reference material as is available, as the subject has not received any great coverage in Western languages.

The system of relating military tactics to the eight trigrams is known as the *Pa Chên*, the 'Eight Arrays' or 'Eight Formations'. It may well be a mark of its obscurity that even the 'Kuei Ku Tzu' book on occult strategy is silent on the subject[2].

The earliest reference to suggest the use of any such system concerns King Kou Chien of Yüeh, and has already been mentioned briefly. Kou Chien has a reputation as a strategist quite independent of any relation to the trigrams. Defeated in a war with the neighbouring state of Wu, Kou Chien quietly rebuilt his own kingdom while working to corrupt the ministers at the court of Wu. His master stroke, however, was to send the beautiful Hsi Shih as a slave to King Fu Ch'a of Wu. Hsi Shih has since become an archetypal figure of feminine beauty in China, and Fu Ch'a became besotted with her to the detriment of state affairs. Weakened through such neglect, Wu was conquered by Kou Chien in 472 BC[3].

The reference linking this famous strategist with the eight trigrams occurs in the *Shih Chi* (Historical Records) of Ssǔ-ma Chien, written toward the end of the second century BC[4]. Chapter 127, 'Biographies of the Diviners of Lucky Days', is almost entirely given over to a speech by a certain Ssǔ-ma Chi-chu. This worthy divined in the market-place of the Han capital, Ch'ang-an, during the reign of Emperor Wên (179–156 BC). The diviner says: 'Kou Chien, the King of Yüeh, by imitating the eight trigrams of King Wên, was able to defeat his enemies and become one of the dictators of China'. This could be taken as simply implying that Kou Chien was a master of divination, and was thus able to defeat his enemies.

However, the word 'imitating' does seem to suggest some form of patterning based on the trigrams, and their use in battlefield tactical formations cannot be ruled out. Nor can the possibility of anachronism for, as has already been shown, it is by no means certain that the trigrams were in existence as early as Kou Chien's time, in the fifth century BC. It may well be that a later tactical system has been attributed to a famous strategist and tactician of earlier times. If nothing else, though, the reference does show that the trigrams and military affairs were linked in the thought of the last decades of the second century BC, when Ssǔ-ma Chien wrote his history. As pointed out in Chapter 4, the 'trigrams of King Wên' may or may not refer specifically to the World of the Senses arrangement. Nevertheless, references to this arrangement will recur when the use of the Eight Arrays is examined in their more fully developed form.

It is in the Later Han dynasty that references to the *Pa Chên* as such first appear. Professor Derk Bodde has collected three rather obscure references from this period. The most important of these is a quotation from a memorial submitted by un-named 'civil officials' to Ts'ao Ts'ao in AD 216. Ts'ao was at the time the King of Wei and the true power behind the throne; the last Han emperor was no more than a puppet, and Ts'ao's son established the state of Wei in the succeeding Three Kingdoms Period. The memorial is quoted in the commentary to the *San Kuo Chih*, the official History of the Three Kingdoms[5]. Its subject was the Grand Military Review of the army and horse carried out in the tenth lunar month. Bodde translates as follows[6]: 'Soldiers of the assembled Five Battalions would perform the advances and retreats of the 'eight formations', and this was called *shêng-chih*'.

The Five Battalions (*Wu Ying*, sometimes translated as Five Regiments) composed the Northern Army, the central military power of the Later Han. They were stationed at the capital, Lo-yang, and comprised: the Garrison Cavalry, the Elite Cavalry, the Chang River Regiment, the Archers Who Shoot at a Sound, and the Footsoldiers. Each unit consisted of some 800 men[7]. An assembly of all these battalions would give a total of 4,000 men, which would seem an inordinately large number to carry out display exercises for a military review. Perhaps only a smaller, representative group were involved. From the above quotation, however, it is by no means certain whether the advances and retreats of the Eight Formations were carried out by infantry, or horse, or both. A clue is provided by the term *shêng-chih*, but we shall return to this shortly, after looking at Bodde's other references.

The next passage comes from the 'Treatise on Ritual' in the *Hou Han Shu*, the official History of the Later Han dynasty. This treatise was written by Ssŭ-ma Piao (AD 240–306). The reference is to military exercises carried out at another festival, the Ch'u-liu sacrifice, and Bodde's translation reads[8]: 'The drilling by troops and officers in the 64 formations of the art of war of Sun and Wu is known as *shêng-chih*'.

Sun and Wu are Sun Wu (sixth to fifth centuries BC) and Wu Ch'i (c. 440–381 BC). Both men were authors of famous treatises on the art of war; however, neither work contains any reference to the Eight Arrays, or to 64 formations[9]. Bodde is of the opinion that the formations mentioned here are 'military exemplifications of the 64 hexagrams', while the Eight Arrays refer to the eight trigrams.

Bodde's final passage comes from a commentary on one of the Books of Rites, the *Li Chi*. According to the *Li Chi*, military exercises are held in the tenth month, in which the troops practice archery, charioteering and feats of strength. The commentary, by Lu Chih (died AD 192) says[10]: 'These feats of strength include ones like *Shêng-chih*, "drawing the bow" and "football".'

Chinese 'football' is a game in which several players attempt to keep a light wicker ball in the air, using only their feet. In this context, it would appear that *shêng-chih* is to be thought of as more of a skill, rather than as a feat of *strength* as such. But what is *shêng-chih*?

Bodde admits to uncertainty[11]. *Shêng* (also pronounced *ch'êng*) can mean a chariot, or to ride, to drive, and so forth. *Chih* is usually a pronoun or a possessive. Bodde therefore speculates that the phrase may mean 'to ride or drive them (or it)', but wonders if the term is an abbreviation, or whether it should be written differently.

I would like to suggest an alternative solution. *Chih* has another, rarer meaning, based on the shape of the written character, which is very similar to the English 'Z'. This meaning is 'zigzag' or 'winding'. *Shêng-chih* would thus mean 'riding zigzag' or 'riding in a winding path'. This would appear to be much more applicable to a skilled display of military manoeuvring involving the advance and retreat of eight (or 64) formations of troops. It would also imply that the Eight Arrays are equestrian manoeuvres. As we shall see, however, this remains a moot point. It is possible that the Eight Arrays may have been performed by either infantry or horse; perhaps the actual *pattern* of the manoeuvres is the most important point.

It is possible that something similar is being described in a poem by Yang Hsiung, although here the manoeuvres appear to be carried out by infantry. Yang Hsiung (53 BC–AD 18) was the author of the *T'ai Hsüan Ching*, an imitation of the *I Ching* which added a third variable to the usual yang and yin, that of *hsüan*, 'the mysterious'. This work is based on the numerology of nine and has 81 tetragrams with nine judgements each. It is an extremely obscure work which did not attain a great circulation and was not particularly well thought of during the Han dynasty. Yang Hsiung is remembered much more as a poet. The poem concerned here is the 'Sweet Springs Rhapsody', probably composed in 11 BC. The language of this type of poem is extremely ornate and difficult, given to lush metaphors and extreme exaggeration. The relevant passage appears to describe a set of military exercises in extravagant and supernatural terms. However, in line with the conventions of this sort of poem, the participants are stellar spirits, said to be under the control of a constellation known as the Angular Array (*Kou Chên*). Knechtges translates as follows:

> 'The Eight Spirits race off, warning the people to clear the road; raising a thunderous clamour, they don their martial attire. Warriors like Ch'ih-yu, girded with Kan Chiang swords, grasping jade axes, fly hurry-scurry, run helter-skelter. Evenly grouped and gathered, they are compactly commingled. Swift as whirlwinds, fleet as clouds, they disperse in all directions. They are ranged in ranks, arrayed in columns, like rows of fishscales, heaped one upon the other. Then, in ragged lines, jagged files, they leap like fish, glide like birds. Radiant and resplendent, swift and sudden, they gather like fog, close in like mist; then, they scatter and spread, casting off lustre, brilliantly creating an elegant pattern' [12].

Ch'ih-yu is a legendary rebel, renowned for his ferocity; Kan Chiang was a swordsmith of Kou Chien's day, whose blades were considered to be masterpieces. It can hardly be said with certainty that this passage, under its poetic metaphors, describes the Eight Arrays. However, certain phrases used here reappear in later descriptions of the Eight Arrays, which will be discussed shortly. There is no mention of horses or other mounts here; the passage may be describing an infantry manoeuvre.

It is at the end of the Han dynasty that we meet the acknowledged master of the Eight Arrays, Chu-ko Liang (AD 181–234). He lived in a period of great turbulence. By about AD 200 the Han empire was in a state of collapse, torn apart by the religious rebellion of the Taoist Yellow Turbans, and by the power-struggles of local warlords. The warfare continued for another 20 years before the Han rule was finally dissolved in name as well as fact, to be replaced by the 'Three Kingdoms' of Wei in the North, Wu in the South-East, and Shu in the South-West. These kingdoms, in turn, continued to war amongst themselves until Wei conquered both Shu, in AD 265, and Wu in AD 280.

In AD 208 Chu-ko Liang joined a minor prince of the Han line, Liu Pei, to whom he had been recommended as a master of military strategy. He proved himself exemplary not only in strategy but also in politics and government, and became prime minister of Shu when Liu Pei established that kingdom in AD 221. Chu-ko Liang was also an inventor of some repute. A particular type of multi-shot siege-crossbow is attributed to him, as are 'Wooden Oxen and Flying Horses'. These are traditionally said to be automata moving under their own power, which he used for transporting military supplies[13]. Later Chinese tradition has made Chu-ko Liang the archetypal 'military genius', near omniscient, inventing strange devices and baffling his opponents at every turn. This tradition may, for all we know, have originated in the military propaganda of his own lifetime. The name by which he was referred to in polite society was K'ung Ming ('Greatly Enlightened'), but he was commonly known as Wo Lung, the 'Sleeping Dragon'. After his death he was given the posthumous title Wu Hou, the 'Martial Marquis', and temples were dedicated to his memory. One such temple exists to this day in Ch'êng Tu, although the building itself was not erected until the T'ang dynasty[14]. A woodblock portrait of Chu-ko Liang is shown in Figure 32.

Such was Chu-ko Liang's reputation that a certain amount of folklore has become attached to his name. He has become a popular figure in later Chinese romance where, in addition to his other guises, he has become a magician besides. This may derive from the fact that he was also adopted by certain Taoist sects as one of their founding worthies, and his name has been attached to several teachings on magic ritual.

He is also closely associated with divination, and is alleged to be the inventor of an oracle system known as the Five Golden Pennies[15]. This uses five coins to develop a five-line figure or pentagram, similar to an *I Ching* hexagram though rather more primitive. Such a pentagram has no moving lines and is incapable of transforming into a second figure. As will be seen in the following pages, Chu-ko Liang appears to have been quite familiar with the *I Ching* and it is difficult to see why he should have been interested in a simpler and less sophisticated system; later attribution has to be suspected once more.

Chu-ko Liang is also credited with the invention of a complicated divination method based on the number of brush-strokes used to write a name in Chinese. This number is then used to find one of a set of hidden verses which lie concealed in a long and apparently meaningless text[16]. The text appearing in modern almanacs is undoubtedly a recent production, as there are references to tobacco and opium which were only introduced to China in recent centuries; the actual method of divination may, of course, be older. In passing

Figure 32
Chu-ko Liang, shown in the wheeled carriage that he was forced to use in later life as a result of illness.

it might be noted that the number of hidden verses is 384; exactly the same number as the total of the individual line judgements attached to the *I Ching* hexagrams. No other connection between the two oracles is immediately apparent, however.

The writings of Chu-ko Liang, on a variety of subjects, survive in fragmentary form in the *Chu-ko Liang Chi*, a collection of pieces put together in the Ch'ing dynasty by Chang Shu[17]. These fragments are all that remain of an original 'collected writings' of

Chu-ko Liang, said to run to 104,112 words and bearing the same title; the original collection has been lost.

The folklore surrounding his name adds an element of difficulty to the task of picking out the factual material relating to Chu-ko Liang and his association with the Eight Arrays. Eventually we shall have to have recourse to just such legendary material in search of clues. However, there are some discoveries to be made in more fully-authenticated source material, and that will be dealt with first.

The official history of the period is disappointingly lacking in detail, although this is not unexpected. The period was chaotic and the kingdom of Shu, where Chu-ko Liang lived and worked, is particularly poorly documented. It has been said that Shu did not establish a government history bureau and 'no one was in charge of note-taking and record-keeping'[18]; however, the exact state of Shu historiography is still a matter of some scholarly dispute.

What we now possess as the official 'History of the Three Kingdoms' has a curious history in itself. It began as a private history, the *San Kuo Chih*, written by Ch'ên Shou (AD 233–297). In AD 428, P'ei Sung-chih was commissioned to write a commentary on Ch'ên's work, which he presented to the throne the following year. The resulting amalgam of Ch'ên's history and P'ei's commentary has been preserved in all editions of the Official Histories ever since[19].

In the *San Kuo Chih* Ch'ên Shou wrote a biography of Chu-ko Liang, which he completed in AD 274, only 40 years after his subject's death. There the following brief reference is to be found: 'By nature, (Chu-ko) Liang was good at inventions; the *sun-i* ('decrease and increase') conjoined crossbow and wooden oxen and flying horses were entirely his idea; in practicing the art of war, the Eight Arrays formation answered all his purposes'[20]. There are no other details, although it might be noted here that the implication is that Chu-ko Liang actually used the Eight Arrays on the battlefield, rather than simply as manoeuvres carried out for display purposes at military reviews.

All else apart, this is good historical evidence that Chu-ko Liang actually practiced the Eight Arrays. Ch'ên Shou was a native of Shu and after the fall of that kingdom he was specially commissioned to record Chu-ko Liang's story[21]. Ch'ên's father had held a post under the Shu general Ma Su. When Ma Su disobeyed orders and suffered a military defeat in AD 228, Chu-ko Liang had him executed and degraded Ch'ên's father to convict status. Ch'ên Shou himself was a contemporary of Liang's son, Chu-ko Chan, although the relationship between the two men seems to have been one of enmity rather than friendship, which is perhaps understandable under the circumstances[22]. In his writings, Ch'ên is occasionally critical of Chu-ko Liang, which would seem to make him a credible witness as far as the Eight Arrays is concerned. Ch'ên would have no reason to glorify the genius of a family enemy by embellishing his military prowess.

Both the *T'ung Chih* ('Historical Collections', by Chang Ch'ien, c. AD 1150), and the bibliographical chapter of the *History of the Sung Dynasty* (written c. AD 1345), mention the existence of a volume on the Eight Arrays written by Chu-ko Liang[23]. No such work is mentioned by Ch'ên Shou, who gives a bibliographical list of 24 works by Chu-ko Liang known to him[24]. This makes the Sung dynasty references rather puzzling. If the book did not exist in Ch'ên's time, the possibility arises that it may be a forgery composed sometime between the third and twelfth centuries; as the book has apparently not survived, there is no way of knowing. Alternatively, Chu-ko Liang's original could possibly have survived in private hands without Ch'ên's knowledge, come into circulation again at a later date, and then been lost once more. Whether forgery or not, the book's loss is certainly regrettable.

The only fragment concerning the Eight Arrays in the present *Chu-ko Liang Chi* is laconic in the extreme. It is a quotation from the *Shui Ching Chu* ('Commentary on the Waterways Classic', by Li Tao-yüan, c. AD 500), which has Chu-ko Liang saying: 'When the Eight Arrays are perfected, the army cannot be defeated'[25].

The same quotation appears in another passage from the *Shui Ching Chu*. This describes a mysterious arrangement of stones on the banks of the Yangtze river at Yü Fu, near the cliff-top city of Pai-ti Ch'êng. The stones are said to have been erected by Chu-ko Liang to display his mastery of the Eight Arrays. The passage is as follows:

'The Yangtze flows east, passing to the south of Chu-ko Liang's display of piled stones at Yü Fu County. Hard against an old military wall that lies to the east (Chu-ko) Liang built the Eight Arrays display with stones dug out from the very edge of the stream, the whole composed of small stones. Going away westward from the wall, the stones are assembled in eight rows, the rows separated by two *chang* (20 Chinese feet), and for this reason they are spoken of as the 'Eight Arrays'. When perfected, the army could not be defeated. All military manoeuvres are hidden in the rows of the display, but men of later times are unable to recognize this'[26].

This display at Yü Fu still exists, although it is by no means certain how good the state of preservation is. As a recent Chinese article says: 'From a high point in the city (Pai-ti Ch'êng) one can look down upon a huge pile of rocks anciently known as "The Fortress of Army Formations" '[27].

Whether Chu-ko Liang actually built the Yü Fu monument or not, it is obvious that his name became attached to it at an early date. Li Tao-yüan was writing only some 250 years after Chu-ko Liang's death. In the same period, according to Li's testimony, the art of how to use the Eight Arrays had been forgotten. Li himself does not appear to have had any great knowledge of the subject, however. The Yü Fu monument does indeed consist of eight rows of piled stones, but this does not appear to be the reason it is spoken of as the Eight Arrays. Rather, it is because representations of the eight trigrams lie concealed amongst the stones, as will become apparent when we come to discuss Figure 33.

The Yü Fu arrangement was by no means the only monument representing the Eight Arrays, although it was the most important. That there were others can be seen from the following passage, from the *Tzŭ Lüeh* of Kao Ssŭ-sun, written about the end of the twelfth century AD.

'Concerning the Eight Arrays formation of Chu-ko Liang, Marquis of Wu-hsiang and prime minister of Shu: one of his displays is by the old wall of Kao Ping, in Mien Yang, but according to Li Tao-yüan's *Shui Ching (Chu)*, it has collapsed and is difficult to recognize. His display at Pa Chên village in Hsin Tu consists of piles of earth, on which are set up stones from the river. This has four gates and two arrangements of 64 heaps each with a 'head'. Each is eight rows by eight rows, made of piles. The total circumference is 472 *pu* (a 'double pace' of five Chinese feet), and there are 130 heaps in all. His formation at Yü Fu, displaying his authority by the Yangtze, is made up of stones as usual. Before it is the gate of a defence wall, and behind it approaches a crescent moon. There are eight vertical and eight horizontal rows of heaps, divided by two *chang* and lying within the arms of the crescent; the whole being in the proportion nine by six and interlocking like the scales of a fish (or, alternatively, "Nines and sixes (yang and yin?) overlapping like scales"). Coming from Min, the Yangtze races along in a raging torrent, swift and startling as sudden thunder, but even this is not enough to oppose its splendour; vast changes occur, but they are not enough to exhaust its strength. For who knows how many years these stones have withstood the shocks around them, yet not one has fallen. Are they not beloved of Heaven? Is this not a mark of divine honour?'[28]

The arrangement at Pa Chên village can be dealt with fairly briefly. It is unusual in being a double arrangement; it might be conjectured that it represents two opposing armies, each drawn up in the Eight Arrays. Each arrangement of 64 heaps is said to have a 'head', but it is unclear precisely what this is. It may be a 65th heap representing the general in command of his army. Some form of additional heap is obviously necessitated by the fact that the total arrangement consisted of 130 such. Whether the 'head' heaps differed in any way from the other heaps remains uncertain.

Some rough idea of the size of the Pa Chên village monument may be gained by assuming it to be a rectangle, twice as long as it is broad. This would seem to be indicated by the fact that it is composed of two square formations next to one another. The circumference is given as 472 *pu*, or 2360 Chinese feet. This would give a rectangle with a short side of 393 feet, a long side of 786 feet. The Chinese foot in Han times being about 9.1 modern inches, in current terms the monument would be about 100 yards by 200.

At Yü Fu, the eight rows of stones are said to be two *chang* apart, so the total width of the square would be about 140 Chinese feet. Converting to modern measurements again, we have a square about 36 yards to each side. The mention of the 'crescent moon' becomes more intelligible when we refer to the diagram of the Yü Fu arrangement given in Figure 33. This comes from the *Wu Pei Chih*[29], ('Records of War Preparations'), a military treatise written by Mao Yüan-I in AD 1628. Here, at the foot of the diagram, there is a crescent formation of black squares, linked together in four groups of six and captioned 'Twenty-four arrays of cavalry'. These obviously correlate with the 'crescent moon', though whether they are represented on the ground at Yü Fu by heaps of stones or by a natural feature of the landscape is uncertain. With the addition

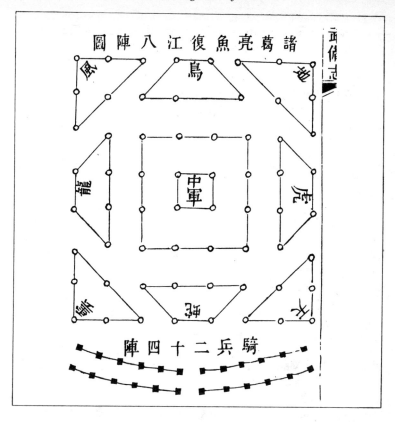

Figure 33
From the seventeenth century Wu Pei Chih. The top caption reads:
'Chu-ko Liang's Yü Fu river Eight Arrays Formation'. The centre:
'Central Army'. Outer ring, reading clockwise from the middle of the
left side: 'Dragon, Wind, Bird, Earth, Tiger, Heaven, Snake, Cloud'.
Lowest caption: 'Cavalry: 24 Arrays'.

of the crescent to the square formation, the whole monument
approaches a proportion of nine by six.

In this diagram, the piles of stones are represented by white dots,
here divided into eight groups of six round the perimeter (that
the group at top centre only has five is presumably an error), and
a central cluster of 16. The eight outer groups represent the trigrams,
here captioned with titles that will be shown to correspond to the

World of the Senses arrangement; the square cluster of 16 dots is captioned 'Central Army'. Looking past these artificial groupings, however, it can be seen that the 64 white dots are actually arranged in eight parallel rows of eight, vertically and horizontally; this is exactly as they are described by Li Tao-yüan and Kao Ssŭ-sun.

While it appears that the form of the diagram (the eight rows of eight and the crescent formation) fits in well with the literary descriptions, the question remains as to how accurate are the interpretations? The four cardinal trigrams are here designated by the names of the symbolic animals of the directions; thus Li is represented by the Bird, the animal of the South, and placed at the top of the diagram. This would mean that the crescent moon of cavalry, lying opposite to this, would be in the North. However, Kao states that the arrangement has a defence wall before it and the crescent moon behind; while Li says that the military wall lies to the East. The crescent moon should therefore lie to the West of the array, not to the North of it. It might also be noted that the cavalry here are shown separate from the Eight Arrays themselves. This would seem to imply that the trigrams represent infantry formations, backed up by the cavalry. The Han dynasty evidence, however, implied that the manoeuvres of the Eight Arrays were carried out by cavalry. Perhaps the conclusion to be drawn from all this is that Mao Yüan-I, the author of the *Wu Pei Chih*, had no greater understanding of the Eight Arrays than Li Tao-yüan, 1000 years before him.

Whether Chu-ko Liang actually built all, or any, of the monuments attributed to him can hardly be proved, unless excavation were to reveal material from the third century AD in relation to the sites. He may have built them all. He may have built one, and the other monuments are imitations that have been attributed to him. It is also possible that he built none of them and that all the monuments had an independent existence of their own before being attributed to Chu-ko Liang. Such a rationalistic explanation has been offered regarding the monument at Yü Fu: that it perhaps consists of megaliths from very early times[30]. This proposal seems to have been made in ignorance of the fact that there are other similar sites besides Yü Fu, and the proposer refers to the formation as consisting of 'great stones'. That they were not, but rather heaps of small stones, has already been shown. Besides, there seems to be little or no evidence for a megalithic culture in

China corresponding to that which in western Europe produced Stonehenge and similar monuments. Furthermore, the use of the number 64 would appear to suggest at least some knowledge of the *I Ching* on the part of the builders. As it has been shown that the *I Ching* is a product of mature Chinese civilization, this would give a date incompatible with megalithic culture. Lastly, knowledge of the *I Ching* would suggest that the builders were of the majority Han nationality, rather than a more primitive megalith-building minority.

Such arguments, though, depend on the assumption that the number 64 is directly, rather than coincidentally, related to the *I Ching*. The traditional material to follow very much suggests that the relationship is direct, but let us review the early factual material presented so far. Leaving aside the diagram from *Wu Pei Chih*, which has a late, seventeenth century, origin and may have been contaminated by traditional material, there has been no direct linkage between the Eight Arrays and the eight trigrams. The most suggestive point is that the Han dynasty references mention that *shêng-chih* is performed in relation to both the Eight Arrays and to 64 formations; but neither trigrams nor hexagrams are mentioned in the texts themselves. From the same sources we know that the Eight Arrays were performed as exercises in military reviews, and from Ch'ên Shou we know that Chu-ko Liang used the Arrays on the battlefield. Li Tao-Yüan and Kao Ssŭ-sun describe *Pa Chên* monuments of 64 heaps arranged in a square, eight rows by eight. This is a consistent body of tradition, but still there is no mention of the trigrams.

From a sceptical point of view, it might be suggested that originally the Eight Arrays had nothing to do with the trigrams or the *I Ching*. Such a suggestion would suppose that later tradition had then reinterpreted the early evidence to weave a fantasy of the eight trigrams and 'occult strategy'; and perhaps forged a book on the subject, attributed to Chu-ko Liang. Such a view cannot be discounted completely, of course. However, the traditional material is also generally consistent, even if there are occasional discrepancies in detail. Our attention must now turn to this material in search of further clues.

The major source of traditional material on the Eight Arrays is the *San Kuo Chih yen-i*, the 'Romance of the Three Kingdoms'. The first version of this was written about AD 1370 by Lo Kuan-chung, but his work was considerably revised in the seventeenth century by Mao Tsung-kang. This vast novel claims to be a popularization of the *San Kuo Chih* of Ch'ên Shou, and is perhaps 70 per cent factual[31]; the remaining 30 per cent consists of popular oral tradition and novelistic embellishment. This hardly makes it the most reliable source material, but many of its references can be correlated with other sources to give a good idea of the *tradition* relating to the Eight Arrays, if not the hard facts.

The first passage from the *Romance* that mentions the Eight Arrays concerns the stones at Yü Fu[32]. These it sees as not merely a monument to Chu-ko Liang's mastery of a near-magical strategy, but as containing some of that magic in themselves. The passage can be summarized as follows:

The army of Shu, having been defeated by the general Lu Hsün of the Wu Kingdom, was retreating along the Yangtze toward Pai-ti Ch'êng. Pursuing them, Lu Hsün came to a halt, remarking that he saw an aura of death ahead and feared an ambush. Scouts were dispatched ahead, finding no troops, but '80 or 90' heaps of boulders on the river bank (the *Wu Pei Chih* diagram shows 64 heaps and 24 arrays of cavalry: 88 in all).

The local inhabitants were summoned, who informed Lu Hsün that when Chu-ko Liang was retreating he and his soldiers heaped up the boulders, and that they had seen 'vapours' rising from them. Deciding to inspect the boulders himself, Lu Hsün rode off with a small escort. Looking down at the heaps from a slope, he saw that they were arranged with four faces related to the eight points of the compass, and they had gates (*Mên*) and doors.

'This looks likely to drive a man out of his senses', said Lu Hsün (a remark with which it is possible to feel a great deal of sympathy!). Nonetheless, he and his men rode down amongst the stones. Dusk was falling and it was decided to return to camp; but as they looked for an exit a sudden squall came on and the dust whirled up, obscuring sky and earth. The stones seemed to rear up like steep mountains, pointed like swords, and the dust and sand shaped themselves into waves and hillocks. The roar of the river was like the drums before a battle.

Lu Hsün lost his way and was unable to find an exit. He had given himself up to lamentation when an old man appeared and led him out of the formation. This scene is shown in Figure 34 where the artist has, perhaps for the sake of simplicity, shown the

Figure 34
Lu Hsün being rescued from the Eight Arrays by Chu-ko Liang's father-in-law. By an anonymous artist, from a block-print edition of The Romance of the Three Kingdoms published in the early Ch'ing dynasty. The caption reads: 'The stones of the Eight Arrays formation ambush Lu Hsün'.

Arrays as eight single boulders. The newcomer turned out to be
Chu-ko Liang's father-in-law, and he told Lu Hsün that the stones
represented the Eight Arrays. There were eight gates, named:

> The Gate of Rest,
> The Gate of Life,
> The Gate of Injury,
> The Gate of Obstruction,
> The Gate of Prospect,
> The Gate of Death,
> The Gate of Surprise,
> The Gate of Openings.

He added: 'They are capable of infinite mutations and would
be equal to 10 legions of soldiers'.

Despite receiving instructions that if any general of Wu became
trapped within the stones he was not to lead him out, the old man
had seen Lu Hsün enter by the Gate of Death, and guessed that
he was ignorant of the scheme. Being soft-hearted and unable to
bear the thought of Lu Hsün being trapped without possibility
of escape, he had come to guide him to the Gate of Life. Even so,
his knowledge was slight. The variations of the scheme were
inexhaustible and he could not learn them all. Thanking the man,
Lu Hsün rode away and gave up the pursuit of the army of Shu.

It is recorded in the histories[33] that Liu Pei led an expedition
against Wu in AD 222, and that the incursion was driven off by
Lu Hsün. The army of Shu then retreated along the Yangtze to
Pai-ti Ch'êng. However, there is nothing to suggest that Chu-ko
Liang was actually present on this campaign, nor is there any
mention of an incident at Yü Fu. However, Lu Hsün did not press
home his advantage, so it is possible that the Yü Fu encounter is
a novelistic explanation of his actions, based on the local traditions
about the Eight Arrays.

Leaving aside such obvious embellishments as the 'vapours' and
the sudden appearance of Chu-ko Liang's father-in-law to provide
an explanation, this is a further strengthening of the tradition that
links the Yü Fu monument with the Eight Arrays. It provides a
story explaining the reason for the building of the monument and
hints strongly at the aura of supernatural power with which the
Eight Arrays were imbued in popular legend. In the same way

that the circular arrangements of trigrams can be used as micro-cosms for magical purposes, so here the Arrays function at a level of non-ordinary reality. They have their origins in the Han magical-cosmological system which does not rely on linear cause and effect; operations can be carried out by the manipulation of symbols to produce effects laterally through the connected web of correlations and resonances. This adds an extra dimension to the simple equestrian manoeuvring of several units of troops for tactical purposes mentioned in earlier references. Those units have now become the symbols manipulated by a magician-general, and the effects produced have a supernatural potency beyond the ordinary physical reality of men and weapons and manoeuvres. In this case, indeed, these supernatural effects are thought to have enough of an independent existence as to allow them to be transferred to an array of stones while still retaining their potency.

This passage is typical of the folklore that attributes a more-than-natural genius to Chu-ko Liang. However, it also provides us with our first information on the actual patterning used in the Eight Arrays. They are said to correspond to the same eight gates as were found in the 'Devil Valley Diagram' discussed in the last chapter. The Gates are here given in precisely the same order as found in that diagram; there the order is given clockwise, reading round from a starting position in the North.

The second passage from the *Romance*[34] brings the Eight Arrays onto the actual battlefield. The armies of Shu and Wei were drawn up by the banks of the Wei river. After some negotiation between Chu-ko Liang and the Wei general Ssŭ-ma I, a contest of battle-arrays was proposed; a dual of tactics before the onset of major hostilities. The contest was opened by Ssŭ-ma I, who drew up his men in the *Hun yüan i ch'i* formation. Brewitt-Taylor, perhaps wisely, leaves this untranslated. It appears to mean something along the lines of 'Mixed troops united under one leader' or 'Mixed troops operating as one'; mixed troops in this case referring to a formation consisting of both infantry and cavalry. Regrettably, further information on this form of battle array is lacking. It was, however, greeted with derision by Chu-ko Liang, who then drew up his own formation.

Having declared that he recognized the formation as the *Pa Kua Chên* (Eight Trigrams Array), Ssŭ-ma I was then invited to attack it. He chose three of his captains, each to lead 30 horsemen, and gave them a briefing which Brewitt-Taylor translates as follows:

> That formation consists of eight gates of well-known names. You
> will go in from the East at the Gate of Life, turn to the South-West
> and make your way out by the Gate of Destruction. Then enter
> at the North, at the Open Gate, and the formation will be broken
> up. But be cautious.

Regrettably, there is a mistranslation here. The relevant part of
the Chinese text actually reads: 'You three men will force an entry
at the eastern Gate of Life, turn towards the South-West and fight
your way out of the Gate of Rest, return and fight your way in
through the Gate of Openings at the North'.

This passage presents a number of problems, but let us first see
how the attack turned out. The captains and their men entered
the Gate of Life, to the applause of both sides. Yet having entered,
they found themselves facing a wall of troops and could not find
their way out. They hastened round the base of the line toward
the South-West, intending to exit there, but were stopped by a flight
of arrows. Becoming confused, they saw many gates and lost their
bearings, dashing to and fro, lost as if in a mist. Then a shout rose,
and each man was seized and bound. They were taken to the central
army where Chu-ko Liang had his tent. However, after depriving
them of their weapons and horses he released them, sending them
back to Ssŭ-ma I with a message that he needed to study further.

Even disregarding Brewitt-Taylor's mistranslation, Ssŭ-ma I's
briefing is still full of errors. As can be seen from the 'Devil Valley
Diagram', the Gate of Life is in the North-East, not the East. The
Gate of Rest is actually in the North, not the South-West; and the
Gate of Openings is in the North-West, not the North. Quite
obviously the author of the *Romance* is trying to tell us that
Ssŭ-ma I was a bumbler who failed to understand even the simplest
directional aspects of the Eight Arrays; thus Chu-ko Liang's message
that he needed to study further.

However, there is still a further problem. Ssŭ-ma I's captains are
said to have entered the Gate of Life, presumably by following their
briefing and going in from the East, to the applause of both sides.
This would seem to imply that the Gate of Life was actually in
the East, not the North-East. A possible explanation for this
apparent contradiction presents itself in the *Wu Pei Chih* diagram.

There the Eight Arrays are given names such as Heaven, Earth, Wind and so forth, which will be shown to correspond to the trigrams of the World of the Senses arrangement. Four of these trigram names are derived from the animals of the cardinal points, thus indicating that the trigrams are arranged in relation to the eight points of the compass. From the 'Devil Valley Diagram' it has been seen that the Eight Gates are also directionally designated according to the same eight compass points. Thus the North-West Gate of Opening corresponds with Heaven, or Ch'ien. In the *Wu Pei Chih* diagram, the trigrams are shown at the corners and sides of the array. This obviously results from the fact that the formation as a whole is square, rather than octagonal.

However, there are openings *between* the clusters of stones representing the trigrams. At least as far as the Yü Fu monument is concerned it is possible that it was these openings which were thought to represent the Gates, rather than the clusters of stones representing the trigrams. If these openings do represent the Gates, however, it will be seen that they fall only on the *sides* of the square, two per side. It would thus be difficult to specify a 'North-East' gate, because in that general direction there would be two Gates, one on the northern side of the square, one on the eastern. If it were then to be assumed that the Gate corresponding to a particular trigram was that opening which lies immediately next to it in a clockwise direction, Ssŭ-ma I's briefing would start to make a little more sense. The Gate of Life, normally positioned in the North-East, would then lie on the eastern side of the square, as Ssu-ma I says, but toward the northern end of that side. Similarly, the Gate of Openings, normally said to lie in the North-West, would lie on the northern side of the square, toward the western end. Looked at in this way, there is only one major error in Ssŭ-ma I's briefing which proved his undoing. That is the wrong placing of the Gate of Rest, which would lie on the northern side of the square, toward the eastern end; there would be no need for his men to travel toward the South-West in order to find it.

There is no mention here of whether Chu-ko Liang's troops, forming the Arrays, were infantry or cavalry. That the attacking captains met a 'wall of troops' might suggest that they were infantry. In such a case it is possible that the author was following the same tradition as the *Wu Pei Chih* diagram in separating the cavalry from the Arrays. Further evidence of a shared tradition would seem to be that the diagram shows a Central Army, and the same feature appears in the middle of the Array in the novel. Quite logically, Chu-ko Liang's tent is placed there; the commander would hardly leave himself open to attack at the centre of the formation without a protective array of troops. The commander's tent itself may perhaps correspond to the 'head' mentioned in the description of the arrays at Pa Chên village. The extra, sixty-fifth heap, perhaps placed at the centre of the array, could correspond to the general commanding the army.

The fact that at one point the attacking captains met a flight of arrows might suggest that each trigram group was armed with different weapons, but unfortunately there is no further information to confirm this. Similarly, that they unexpectedly met a wall of troops might suggest that the formation was being manoeuvred tactically while the attack was occurring. Again, the text provides no further clues.

Such tactical manoeuvring is mentioned, however, in the third passage from the *Romance*[35]. This brings us to the subject of 'working evolutions' with the Eight Arrays. The term used in the novel is *p'ien hua* ('transformations', 'evolutions'). There is no mention of *shêng chih*; it is possible that the term might have dropped out of use by the time the novel was written.

The episode recorded in this passage occurred after Chu-ko Liang's death. His teachings (in the form of a book, it is to be noted) had passed to his successor, Chiang Wei. His opponents, at a place called Ch'i Shan, were once again the men of Wei, this time led by Têng Ai and Ssŭ-ma Wang. Chiang Wei drew up his men in the Eight Arrays which, rather than being designated as Gates, are here referred to as Heaven, Earth, Wind, Cloud, Bird, Serpent, Dragon and Tiger. These names correspond precisely with those given to the Arrays in the *Wu Pei Chih* diagram.

These names designate the trigrams in the World of the Senses arrangement. They are listed in two groups. The first four refer to the trigrams lying on the diagonals, which the *I Wei* refer to as *Mên*, 'Gates'. Heaven is Ch'ien, Earth K'un, and Wind is Sun. However, there is some mystery as to why the term 'Cloud' has been attributed to Kên (Mountain). Cloud would more normally be an attribute of Tui; perhaps some strained explanation of 'clouds round peaks' is possible for its attribution to Kên. The second group corresponds to the trigrams designated *Chêng* ('Pillars') by the *I*

Wei, and they are here named after the symbolic animals of the directions. Bird (South) is Li; Serpent (North) is K'an; Dragon (East) is Chên; Tiger (West) is Tui. The various systems of Gates, trigrams, directions and names are correlated in the following table:

Mên	HEAVEN	Ch'ien	North-West	Gate of Opening
Mên	EARTH	K'un	South-West	Gate of Death
Mên	WIND	Sun	South-East	Gate of Obstruction
Mên	CLOUD	Kên	North-East	Gate of Life
Chêng	BIRD	Li	South	Gate of Prospect
Chêng	SERPENT	K'an	North	Gate of Rest
Chêng	DRAGON	Chên	East	Gate of Injury
Chêng	TIGER	Tui	West	Gate of Surprise

Têng Ai recognized Chiang Wei's formation and drew up a corresponding one of his own. However, Chiang Wei then challenged him to work variations with the Arrays. Têng Ai returned to his ranks, gave his signal officers certain orders, and evolved the 'eight eights' of the variations in rapid succession.

These concluded satisfactorily, Chiang next challenged him to a surrounding move. Têng's tactics 'did not grip' and then, at a signal from Chiang, the troops of Shu transformed the Eight Arrays to surround Têng and his men, using the *Ch'ang shê chüan ti chên.* Literally, this means 'a long snake curled on the ground formation'. Têng Ai was at the point of surrender when reinforcements from Wei, led by Ssŭ-ma Wang, dashed up from the North-West and rescued him. Despite this, Têng's nine camps were captured and he retreated south of the Wei river.

Ssŭ-ma Wang thereupon explained that he had recognized Chiang Wei's Serpent Formation, and that the only way to break it was to attack the head of the snake, which he saw was in the North-West. The importance of this Serpent Formation, and its direct connection to the Eight Arrays, will become apparent shortly, when we turn our attention to Taoist magic.

It was decided that the next day Ssŭ-ma Wang would hold Chiang Wei's attention with another contest of tactics while Têng Ai took a force to attack from the rear, and a challenge was duly issued. On its receipt, however, Chiang Wei told his officers that he possessed a secret book from Chu-ko Liang which contained 365 variations of the Eight Arrays, corresponding to the circuit of the heavens. The challenge from the army of Wei was seen to be preposterous, and doubtless a ruse. Chiang Wei therefore took counter-measures against an attack from the rear.

The following morning the two armies were drawn up and Ssŭ-ma Wang, as challenger, was the first to display his tactics. He made the Eight Arrays and, on being challenged, announced that the variations he knew numbered 'nine nines, making 81'. Ssŭ-ma Wang then demonstrated many such variations, before riding out to ask if Chiang Wei recognized them. His query, however, was met with the following contemptuous reply:

'My formation admits of 365 variations. You are but a frog in a well and know nothing of the deeper mysteries.'

Chiang Wei is quoting a Taoist reference from the philosopher Chuang Tzŭ. In his seventeenth chapter, Chuang tells a parable about a frog that lives in a caved-in well who boasts of the extent of his domain and his mastery over it. He is disabused of his pretentions by the great turtle of the Eastern Sea, who tells him something of the might and vastness of the ocean[36].

Ssŭ-ma Wang, knowing that 365 variations were possible but not having studied them, challenged Chiang Wei to demonstrate. However, Chiang Wei said that he would only demonstrate them to Têng Ai, who was notably absent. The chapter continues with the panic-stricken Ssŭ-ma Wang launching an immediate attack, his defeat, and the failure of Têng Ai's surprise attack; but this is the last that is heard of the Eight Arrays.

What, then, are we to make of these 'variations'? From the references in the *Romance* and the *Wu Pei Chih* diagram, it would appear that the most basic form of the Eight Arrays consists of eight groups of troops. Here there would seem to be a strong possibility that the troops were infantry, rather than the cavalry implied by the Han dynasty references. One possibility to be considered is that Chu-ko Liang's reputation might be based on his having transformed an original set of drill-ground equestrian manoeuvres into a functioning battlefield tactical system using infantry; presumably using the same patterns of manoeuvre and much of the directional terminology of the original. Such a possibility would explain the disappearance of the term *shêng chih*; it is a cavalry term ('riding zigzag') which would not be applicable to infantry. This could explain the term's replacement by the more general *p'ien hua*, 'transformations'. Another possibility, of course, is that whatever Chu-ko Liang's system was had been entirely forgotten, and the tradition reflected in the *Romance* had its origin in a later interpretation based on the Yü Fu monument. All our information on the actual patterning and terminology of the Eight Arrays leads back to Yü Fu and a representation in stone; while Chu-ko Liang's connection with that monument remains unproven, it is impossible to say with certainty that the same patterning and terminology can be traced back to the actual battlefield.

All this aside, the fact that some form of 'variation' or 'mutation' was thought to be possible would seem to imply that these eight units of troops were capable of being moved or reorganized in some way. The most basic form of variation would appear to be that based on the numbers eight and 64. In Chinese, this reads very concisely: 'eight eight 64'. While this could be read in simple arithmetical terms as 'eight times eight makes 64', this would seem to be an unnecessary elaboration. The more likely implication is that the 'eight eights' is the most important part of the phrase, suggesting perhaps eight functions of eight units which, in total, gives 64 variations.

Evidence of these two sets of eight may perhaps be found in the differing terminology applied to the Arrays. At some points they are referred to as Gates, which appear to have strong directional linkages; at others they are referred to by names indicating the trigrams of the World of the Senses arrangement. Possibly these two sets of terminology were not originally interchangeable and indicated different things; perhaps the trigram names were given to the individual units of troops, while the Gates were used to designate their directional positions. If such were the case, it would be simple to make variations of 'eight eights' by merely rotating the entire formation in eight stages of 45 degrees each. This would bring each of the eight trigram units to each of the eight separate positions in turn.

It is possible, however, that something more complex was being attempted than this simple manoeuvring. As the number 64 is mentioned it is possible that the trigram units were somehow manoeuvred to correlate with the 64 hexagrams of the *I Ching*. Such variations could be achieved by a similar simple rotation to that just mentioned, if it was assumed that both the troop units and the positions were designated by trigrams. Let us assume that the unit of troops represents the inner or lower trigram of the hexagram, and the position the outer or upper trigram (or vice-versa). As an example, at the start the Ch'ien unit would be at the Ch'ien position, giving hexagram one, The Creative. At the first rotation (clockwise), the Ch'ien unit would lie at the K'an position, giving hexagram five, Waiting; at the second rotation, hexagram 26, Taming Power of the Great, and so on. Moving all eight units through all eight positions would thus give all 64 possible hexagrams.

These are unprovable speculations, of course; the original manoeuvres may have been more complex. However, from the use of the numbers eight and 64 it is possible to infer that only the eight outer troop units were involved; the ninth, central unit would have played no part in this least difficult form of the manoeuvres. That the second order of difficulty is 'nine nines' becomes more comprehensible if we assume that this central unit or position is involved in the manoeuvres.

It is not entirely impossible that there may be some influence here from the numerology of nine used by the *T'ai Hsüan Ching* of Yang Hsiung; however, this work remained largely a philosophical curiosity, and its influence on the Han correlative system was negligible. There is, besides, a numerology of nine attached to the eight trigrams themselves, quite independent of Yang Hsiung's influence; the magic square of three.

In Chapter 4 the correlation between the World of the Senses arrangement and the Lo Shu square was examined, and we shall return to this shortly in a Taoist magical context. For the moment, though, the magic square gives a purely numerical way of manoeuvring the trigrams. This is based on the 'magic line' of the magic square, as shown in Figure 35.

A further extension of this is the 'Nine Star Circulating Squares', shown in Figure 36. Here the numbers are moved in sequence along the magic line, each moving one place in each variation, to give nine squares. Each number appears at the centre of a square by turn.

This is more easily comprehensible if one looks first at the usual form of the magic square, with five at the centre, which here occupies the central position; and then at the square immediately to its right. Here the number six has moved back along the magic line, from the lower right corner to the central position, while five has moved from the centre to the upper left, and so on. Each number moves into the position that the number preceding it

Figure 35

9	5	7		1	6	8		2	7	9
8	1	3		9	2	4		1	3	5
4	6	2		5	3	7		6	8	4

3	8	1		4	9	2		5	1	3
2	4	6		3	5	7		4	6	8
7	9	5		8	1	6		9	2	7

6	2	4		7	3	5		8	4	6
5	7	9		6	8	1		7	9	2
1	3	8		2	4	9		3	5	1

Figure 36

occupied in the previous square, and this process is repeated for all the numbers in all the squares, always moving along the magic line. When this piece of numerical trickery came into being is uncertain, but it dates back at least to the T'ang dynasty[37]. It is used in certain systems of Chinese 'astrology' (based on cyclical time rather than the motions of the heavenly bodies), particularly in 'Nine House Astrology', which is said to have connections with geomancy[38].

The same system can be used to work variations with the World of the Senses trigrams, as shown in Figure 37. The trigrams, in their normal arrangement, are placed round the normal magic square at the centre of the diagram. The trigrams are then moved along with their correlated numbers, according to the system of the 'Nine Star Circulating Squares'.

Looking once more at the squares with five and six at the centre, it can be seen that K'an, numbered one, moves from the lower centre of square five to the top centre position in square six. The

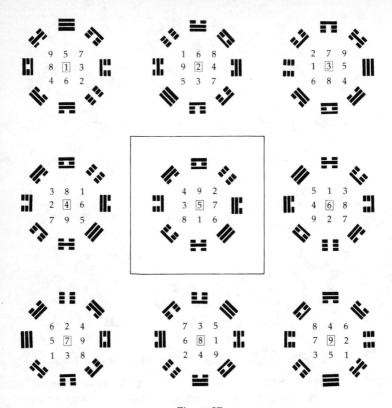

Figure 37

same applies for the first four numbered trigrams. However, as there are nine numbers and only eight trigrams, the number which lies at the centre of each square is not used. Thus Ch'ien, number six in square five, 'slips back' to become number five in square six, and retains this number throughout the rest of the manoeuvres. Tui, numbered seven in square six, gains the number six in square seven, and so on. Thus each of the eight trigrams occupies each of the eight positions in turn. The cycle is completed in square four, which is identical to square five, there being only eight variables, manoeuvred nine times.

There are two ways of interpreting the results of these manipulations. The first is that the eight trigrams have been manoeuvred into eight different positional sets, which provides another way of achieving 'eight eights'. The second is that nine operations have been carried out from start to finish using nine numbers, and this could correspond to the 'nine nines'.

Obviously, such operations would be more than a little difficult to carry out on the battlefield. However, by following the magic line of three in this way, eight groups of horsemen would certainly have to 'ride zigzag', as implied by the phrase *shêng chih*. It has to be re-emphasized, of course, that this interpretation is highly speculative. However, it does show that with enough ingenuity, something which Chu-ko Liang was credited with in abundance, it is *possible* to work 'eight eights' and 'nine nines'.

There remains the final set of variations, numbering 365, 'for the circuit of the heavens'. At first sight this seems utterly preposterous, with no relation to what has gone before. Even so, the idea deserves closer examination.

The division of the circle into 360 degrees was only introduced into China, from the West, about the sixteenth century. Before that the Chinese divided the circle into 365 degrees, basing this on the number of days in the year. It would be possible to divide these degrees further by two, for day and night, or the yang and yin aspects of each day. This would give a figure of 730. It happens that the cube of nine is 729, which is about as close as it is possible to get to 730 without being dead on. Perhaps this is coincidental. However, the idea that the variations can be connected to a series of squares and cubes of the significant numbers eight and nine (64 = eight squared; 81 = nine squared; 729 = nine cubed) could at least suggest some sort of coherent system of numerical thinking. Whether this thinking derives from the authors of the *Romance*, or whether they were transmitting a tradition which goes back to Chu-ko Liang himself is, of course, unanswerable.

Before leaving these numerical speculations, attention might be drawn to a second diagram from the *Wu Pei Chih* book[39], shown in Figure 38. This shows a military array based on the other major arrangement of trigrams, the World of Thought, or Fu Hsi's sequence. It would seem most likely that this is an intruder into the material, and probably the product of a late hand. Even if the World of Thought arrangement existed as early as Chu-ko Liang's day (which is by no means certain), everything else that can be gathered about trigram battle-tactics refers to the World of the Senses sequence. Even so, the presence of the ninth central array

Figure 38
Fu Hsi's Army Trigram Formation. Nine Army Array Formation.

is to be noted, composed of eight yin lines; as is the dot in the centre, presumably representing the commander. It would of course be rash to deny that the World of Thought was ever used tactically, but it seems more likely that this array has been invented to provide a 'balanced set', a World of Thought formation to match that of the World of the Senses. However, the fact that the formation is captioned 'Nine Armies Array' might suggest that it was this formation with which the 'nine nines' variations were worked. It is also possible that the nine components of the central array (the eight yin lines and the dot) might in some way represent the magic square of three; regrettably there is no further information on which to build a theory of explanation.

However, the Gates of the Eight Arrays are normally correlated with the World of the Senses trigrams. While it is well known that this arrangement of trigrams was current in Chu-ko Liang's day, it is necessary to ask whether the Gates themselves existed at that period, and to examine the relationship between the two systems.

It has been pointed out in Chapter 4 that according to the *Ch'ien Tso Tu*, one of the Han dynasty *I Wei* texts, the trigrams lying on the four diagonal directions were known as *Mên*, Gates. Archaeological finds show some evidence of this correspondence between Gates and the diagonals. Loewe tabulates data about six Diviner's Boards which have been recently excavated[40]. Two of these boards have interesting inscriptions on the diagonals of the square Earth plate.

The earlier of the two boards dates from the Earlier Han dynasty. Each of the four inscriptions contain one of the Celestial Stems, either *wu* or *chi*. The direction attributed to both these Stems is that of the Centre; this may have something to do with the fact that the diagonals run from the centre of the board toward the four corners. The inscriptions read as follows:

North-East:	'*Chi* Demon Gate'
South-East:	'*Wu* Earth Gate'
South-West:	'*Chi* Man Gate'
North-West:	'*Wu* Heaven Gate'

There is no mention of the trigrams here, and the system seems to have been drawn up on grounds of opposition across the centre, represented by *wu* and *chi*. The Heaven and Earth Gates oppose each other across one set of diagonals; Man and Demon across the other. This simple system of oppositions may give another contributory factor to the evil reputation of North-East direction.

The second board is later, dating no earlier than the third century AD. This also has inscriptions mentioning the same four Gates, but this time they are connected with four of the trigrams, rather than with the Stems. The inscriptions read:

'North-East Demon Gate, Kên'
'South-East Earth Door, Sun'
'South-West Man Gate, K'un'
'North-West Heaven Gate, Ch'ien'

That the South-East has a Door while the other directions have Gates is curious, but there is no reason apparent for the abberation. Directionally the trigrams are placed according to the World of the Senses arrangement. That Ch'ien has been linked with the Heaven Gate seems quite logical, but the other attributions are more contradictory. One would expect K'un to correspond with the Earth Gate or Door, yet it is linked with the Man Gate. The Earth Gate, meanwhile, is linked with Sun, the Element of which is Wood.

It might be conjectured that the earlier of the two boards contains a Gate-system which, while it might use the term *Mên* to designate the directions, was originally drawn up without reference to the trigrams. It appears to have referred only to a system of opposition across the centre, and was linked to the Celestial Stems. Later, however, it appears that this same system of Gates was applied to the World of the Senses trigrams. The original oppositions seem to have been considered of sufficient importance that they were maintained, even though this led to contradictions with the trigrams.

Although they are linked by the World of the Senses trigrams, the systems of the Eight Arrays and the Diviner's Boards do not correspond well together. In the North-East, the Boards have the Demon Gate, while the Arrays have the Gate of Life and the trigram Cloud. In the South-West, the Boards have the Man Gate, the Arrays the Gate of Death, trigram Earth. There is a curious opposition here of Demon/Life and Man/Death. In the South-East, the Boards have Earth Gate, the Arrays the Gate of Obstruction, trigram Wind; in the North-West the Boards have Heaven Gate, the Arrays the Gate of Opening, trigram Heaven.

In essence, what appears on the Diviner's Boards is a rudimentary system which is *similar* to the Eight Arrays, which can be dated to the Han dynasty. It may share a common origin with the Arrays, but in the absence of further evidence it is impossible to prove that the one derives from the other.

However, although the later of the Diviner's Boards mentioned discards the Celestial Stems when the Gates are linked to the trigrams, the Stems reappear in the divination method of the *Ch'i-mên Tun-chia*, this time in conjunction with the Gates of the Eight Arrays. Before proceeding, a distinction must be made between two different forms of *Tun-chia*. The divination method will be dealt with first; the second form is a 'black' magic ritual.

Ch'i-mên Tun-chia means the 'Mysterious Gates of the Hidden Stems'. As a divination method it has been dated as early as the Han dynasty, and thus it would have been in use during Chu-ko Liang's lifetime; if, indeed he was not responsible for its origination[41]. There is an extant book on the subject, the *Ch'i-mên Tun-chia ch'üan-shu*, the authorship of which is attributed to Chu-ko Liang and Chang Liang[42]. Chang Liang lived at the end of the third and the beginning of the second century BC. He is in some ways a parallel figure to Chu-ko Liang. After a meeting with a mysterious (possibly supernatural) stranger he was given a book, *The Patriarch Lu Shang's Art of War*. After studying this he assisted in the foundation of the Han dynasty, and became strategist and adviser to the first Han emperor[43]. The implication of the dual authorship of the *Tun-chia* book would seem to be that Chang Liang first formulated the system, and that Chu-ko Liang improved it and gave it its final form. The book itself, of course, may be later than either of them.

Regrettably, the *Ch'i-mên Tun-chia* appears to have received little attention in Western languages, although it is easily available in Chinese. Indeed, it is well enough known to be mentioned in martial arts comic-books published in Hong Kong[44]. In full, however, it is an inordinately complicated system. A chapter is devoted to it in the modern work *I Ching Shên-hsüeh* which runs to 90 pages of calculations, tables and charts[45].

The *Tun-chia* divination centres around the Chinese calendrical system of the sexagenary cycle which, as has been seen, uses the Celestial Stems and the Terrestrial Branches. *Chia* is the first of the Celestial Stems; thus the translation of *Tun-chia* as 'hidden stems'. In the magic ritual, however, *chia* refers to the Six *Chia* spirits, but we shall return to this shortly. The purpose of the divination is to discover the dates and directions which are dangerous at certain points in the 60 day cycle. This is interesting, as it is obviously possible to divine for every day of the year; it might be conjectured that Chiang Wei's 365 variations are in some way connected with the *Ch'i-mên Tun-chia*.

Indeed, the 'Mysterious Gates' of the *Ch'i-mên Tun-chia* are those very same eight Gates that we have already found in the Eight Arrays and the 'Devil Valley Diagram'. They are once again correlated with the trigrams in the World of the Senses arrangement, and also with the magic square of three. Here, however, the magic square is given in a celestial version as well as a numerical one, referring to the Nine Stars and the Nine Celestial Palaces. The Nine Stars are those composing the constellation of the Dipper, to which an extra two are added to make up the number. Each star is numbered from one to nine, and they are arranged in a square which corresponds precisely with the magic square of three[46]. The Nine Palaces are those of the god T'ai I, and these are also arranged according to the magic square. Further details will be found in Appendix Three. The *Tun-chia* system also draws correspondences from the Five Elements and seven colours, the colour white appearing three times to bring the number of correspondences up to nine.

The net result is a divination system which, with its use of eights and nines and its correlation with the days of the year, obviously has a considerable relationship with our subject; it is, besides, attributed to Chu-ko Liang himself. Even so, it does seem rather far removed from the actual manipulation of troops on the battlefield. The Taoist magic rituals to be examined next are, however, somewhat more martial in character.

These rituals are the product of the Taoist religion, traditionally founded by Chang Tao-ling in the second century AD, rather than of the ancient philosophical school centred round the works of Lao Tzŭ and Chuang Tzŭ. Although most attention in the West has focussed on the ancient philosophers, the later religion and its enormous canon of scriptures is perhaps a truer reflection of the actual spirit of Chinese Taoism. Indeed, modern scholars have recently begun to refer to Lao Tzŭ and Chuang Tzŭ as 'proto-Taoists'. It should also be said that there is little or no historical evidence to show that Chu-ko Liang had any connection with the Taoist religious movement whatsoever. However, several Taoist sects claim him as one of their early worthies, and we must examine whatever material we find about the Eight Arrays, regardless of which tradition it comes from.

As has already been mentioned briefly, in the *Ch'i-mên Tun-chia* ritual, the word *Chia* refers to the Six Chia sprits. These are violent minor deities who are summoned and brought under control by the magician, who can then call them forth to obey his commands whenever needed. The ritual originates with the Pei-chi (Pole Star) sect of Taoists, who traditionally claim Chu-ko Liang as their founder. The sect originated at a mountain in Hupei called Wu

Tang Shan, where Chu-ko Liang is said to have first practiced the Eight Arrays. Wu Tang is traditionally the home of military magic, and is also a great centre of martial arts[47]. It occupies the same sort of position in the Taoist tradition as the Shaolin monastery does in the annals of the Buddhist fighting arts. However, the ritual discussed here became popular at another great Taoist centre, Mao Shan, in the Sung and Ming dynasties. As a result, its practitioners are often referred to as Mao Shan Taoists.

After 100 days of meditation, a site is chosen for the ritual by a river flowing between two mountains. It might be noted in passing that the presence of a river is a common feature to just about all the references to the Eight Arrays, in battlefield manoeuvres, monuments and magic. The ritual area is set up in a circle of 64 paces, with an altar at the centre. Sixty-four clean stones are selected from an unfrequented spot by the river, or from out of the river itself. The direction of the North-East is found, which represents the Gate of Life, the most important of the Gates used in the ritual. The other seven Gates are then designated, using exactly the same names that have appeared in the previous material. In similar fashion to the first passage from the *Romance of the Three Kingdoms* given above, the list of Gates is given as starting with Rest (trigram K'an), the others following in a clockwise order.

Four of the stones are laid out in a straight line behind each Gate, and similar lines of four are arranged in the intervening spaces. The end result is a radial arrangement of 16 spokes, as shown in Figure 39.

Why this arrangement, which is still called the *Pa Chên*, differs so radically from the others we have observed is not clear. Beyond the Gates are believed to be armies of demons, led by the Six Chia spirits. In a ritual lasting 60 days, using flags of the 28 constellations, written talismans, mantras, mudras and the Paces of Yü, the Taoist summons each of the Six Chia to the Gate of Life, finally gaining power over them all. At a later date they can then be summoned at will, without the need of such extensive preparation, by simply performing the Paces of Yü, or by tracing the numbers of the magic square on the digits of the three major fingers of the left hand. This is an unorthodox ritual, a Tao of the left; what we might call 'black magic'. Full details of the proceedings will be found in Saso[48].

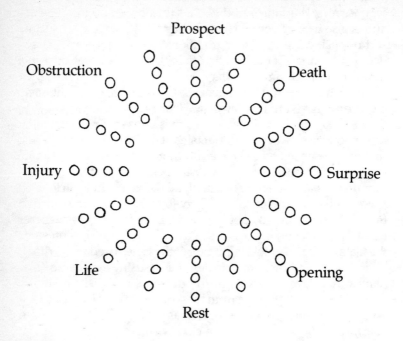

Figure 39 (After Saso)

The Eight Arrays also appear in orthodox Taoist ritual, however. They appear to be a commonplace method of defining the sacred area where rites are performed, and of defining the directions, even when the Arrays are not represented in a physical form. One such use is in the *fa-lu* meditation ritual. Here the disciples enter the area by the Gate of Earth (South-West, here given its name from K'un, Earth, rather than being known as the Gate of Death). The Master, meanwhile, enters through the Gate of Heaven (North-West, named from Ch'ien, rather than being the Gate of Opening). The nomenclature here appears to be purely directional, and the Gates are not physically represented[49].

Further details of the Eight Arrays come from the orthodox Thunder Magic of the Ch'ing-wei sect. The rite cannot be dated before the T'ang dynasty, and it apparently reached its final form during the Sung. Even though comparatively late, it is nonetheless obvious that the system developed in the same tradition as that in which we are interested.

Here is to be found some explanatory material about three of the trigrams in the array, and especially about Kên, the Gate of Life. This is basically a military explanation, in which the shape of the trigrams in the World of the Senses arrangement (Figure 40) is taken as representing the shape of a formation of soldiers.

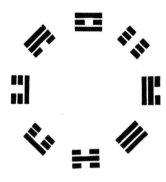

Figure 40

Kên is said to be the weakest position in the circle, because it consists of one strong (yang) line in the outermost position, backed up only by two weak (yin) lines. An attacking general might be expected to burst through the strong outer defence at his first onset, and then to pass on through the two weak defences represented by the yin lines; thus gaining access to the heart of the formation. He would not attack Ch'ien, as it is obviously invulnerable, having three strong yang lines. Nor would he attack K'un as it is too obviously weak and thus suggestive of a hidden ambush. This argument is offered to explain why the Gate of Life is positioned in the inauspicious North-East direction and sometimes named the Gate of Hell. It is the place where matters of life *and* death are decided, and its relevance is to the *whole* of life, rather than just its origin. Its weak position in the circle is thus made to explain why the North-East direction is ritually sealed, and so strengthened, in Taoist ritual [50]. Presumably the same sort of logic could be used to produce arguments about the relative strengths and weaknesses

of the remaining trigrams. For example, it might be conjectured
that Chên would be stronger than Kên because the two weak outer
defences would soak up the energy of an attacker's first onset before
the strong inner defence repelled his thrust.

In Thunder Magic, power is gained over the essence of thunder
by ritual meditation, and then the power is used for various
purposes, from curing illnesses to sealing the Gate of Life in other
rituals. The sacred area must be kept absolutely pure in orthodox
rituals. If an opposing magician were to place, say, one of the violent
Chia spirits within the sacred circle, whatever rite was being
performed would be ruined.

It is the rite that Thunder Magic is specifically used to oppose
that gives our final clues to the Eight Arrays: Mao Shan Snake
Magic[51]. This is a development of the Mao Shan *Ch'i-mên Tun-
chia* rite. Here the trigrams of the Eight Arrays are unwound to
give the form of a snake, as shown in Figure 41. Ch'ien is the trigram
with the most strength, and so it forms the head of the snake. The
other trigrams trail after this in clockwise order, concluding with
Tui at the tail. Ch'ien's link with the head is further strengthened
by the Creative's mobility and striking power. By placing the
appropriate Chia spirit and its army of demon soldiers at Ch'ien,
the snake can then be used to attack the circle of an opposing Taoist
master.

Alternatively, when the need is for defence, the snake chart can
be viewed as a range of hills in which the army units (the trigrams)
are hidden in ambush. Also attached to the chart are a set of oral
instructions which finally give some idea of what the trigrams
represent when thought of as army units; seven of them, at least,

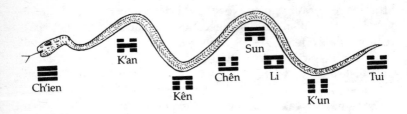

Figure 41 (After Saso)

Kên being omitted for some reason that is not clear. With them go a series of phrases referring to the Five Elements, although the meaning of these is also unclear. They seem to have no connection with the trigrams and their usual Elementary attributions, nor with any sequence of the Five Elements given independently. They are included here for the sake of completeness, and the table is as follows:

Ch'ien	Experienced battle-trained soldiers. Attack!	Wood conquers.
K'an	Hidden soldiers. Ambush.	Water conquers.
Kên	(omitted)	
Chên	Reserve Army.	Fire and Earth conquer.
Sun	Reinforcements.	Wood conquers.
Li	Thunder Brigade. Penetrate deeply.	Metal conquers.
K'un	Defensive Army. Protect and defend.	Water and Earth conquer.
Tui	An army of heroes. Protect and defend.	Water and Earth conquer.

Again, the reasoning behind the attribution of these names to the trigrams is not immediately apparent. Some of them appear logical on the surface: the crack troops at Ch'ien; the ambushing soldiers hidden in K'an, the Abyss; the defensive army at K'un, the Receptive. Why, though, is the Thunder Brigade connected with Li, Lightning, and not Chên, Thunder?

If these matters of detail remain uncertain, it is still obvious that this material fits in with the rest of the tradition that we have examined so far. In the final passage quoted from the *Romance of the Three Kingdoms*, Chiang Wei unwound his Eight Arrays formation into a 'Serpent Coil' with which to attack the opposing commander's Arrays. It is doubtless more than coincidence that the 'head' of Chiang Wei's formation, the only point at which it could be broken, lay in the North-West; this is the direction of Ch'ien, which in the ritual also represents the head of the snake. There are undoubtedly parallels between the novel and the ritual; it appears that a contest of Thunder and Snake Magic has been transferred to the battlefield. The unanswered question remains, of course, whether the authors of the *Romance* had some knowledge of Taoist magic and decided to work it into their plot, or whether both novel and ritual derive from a common source. And if there is a common source, could it definitely be traced back to Chu-ko Liang?

Having come all this way, let us review the material on the Eight Arrays. We have a distinct and consistent body of tradition drawn from monuments, divination, ritual magic and literature. It is known that the Eight Arrays are represented in monuments of 64 heaps of stones, but we do not know how such a stationary monument could represent a movable tactical formation. Some numerical consistency can be seen in the battlefield variations, but we still do not know how those variations worked. There is some information on the names of the army units, and the names of the Gates used to describe their positions, but we still do not know how the units functioned on the battlefield.

The only common factor seems to be that all paths lead back to Chu-ko Liang . . . but alas, both he and his book on the subject have long since vanished in the mists of time.

Appendices

1
The Ma-wang-tui Sequence of the Hexagrams

In Chapter 2 it was pointed out that the commentary known as the *Hsü Kua Chuan*, 'The Sequence of the Hexagrams', is a much later production than the body-text of the *I Ching* itself. It appears to date to a period no earlier than the end of the second century BC. The actual order of the hexagrams in the current edition of the *I Ching*, to which the *Hsü Kua Chuan* refers, does not appear to be that of the original text either. The silk manuscript excavated from the Ma-wang-tui burial of 168 BC treats the hexagrams in a completely different order, which bears no resemblance to the familiar modern sequence.

The ordering of the hexagrams from Ma-wang-tui is beautifully logical, and it is difficult to see why this original system was replaced with the sequence we have today. The system is based on the familial attributes of the trigrams and divides the 64 hexagrams into eight distinct groups, with eight hexagrams in each[1]. These groups are differentiated from one another according to which trigram they have in the upper place. The first group consists of eight hexagrams each having the trigram Ch'ien in the upper position; the second group consists of those having the trigram Kên in the upper place, and so on. These groups are arranged in strict order by sex. The first four feature male trigrams, the second four female, as in the following table:

Upper Trigrams

	Male				Female	
1	Ch'ien	Father		5	K'un	Mother
2	Kên	3rd Son		6	Tui	3rd Daughter
3	K'an	2nd Son		7	Li	2nd Daughter
4	Chên	1st Son		8	Sun	1st Daughter

The lower trigrams in each group of eight also appear in an order based on the familial attributes, but here the male and female trigrams alternate, as follows:

Lower Trigrams

1	Ch'ien	Father		5	K'an	2nd Son
2	K'un	Mother		6	Li	2nd Daughter
3	Kên	3rd Son		7	Chên	1st Son
4	Tui	3rd Daughter		8	Sun	1st Daughter

The first group thus begins with the Creative (Ch'ien in both upper and lower trigram positions) and is followed by Standstill, Retreat, and so on. In the succeeding groups of eight, however, the sequence of lower trigrams is not followed with absolute rigidity; the exception being that each group begins with the hexagram in which the same trigram appears in both the upper and lower places. The second group thus begins with Keeping Still, Kên doubled; the third group with the Abysmal, K'an doubled, and so on. The remaining hexagrams in each separate group, however, continue to run in the same order as the table of lower trigrams given above. This may perhaps be better understood by referring to Figure 42, where the complete sequence of the 64 hexagrams is shown, correlated with their numbers in the current edition.

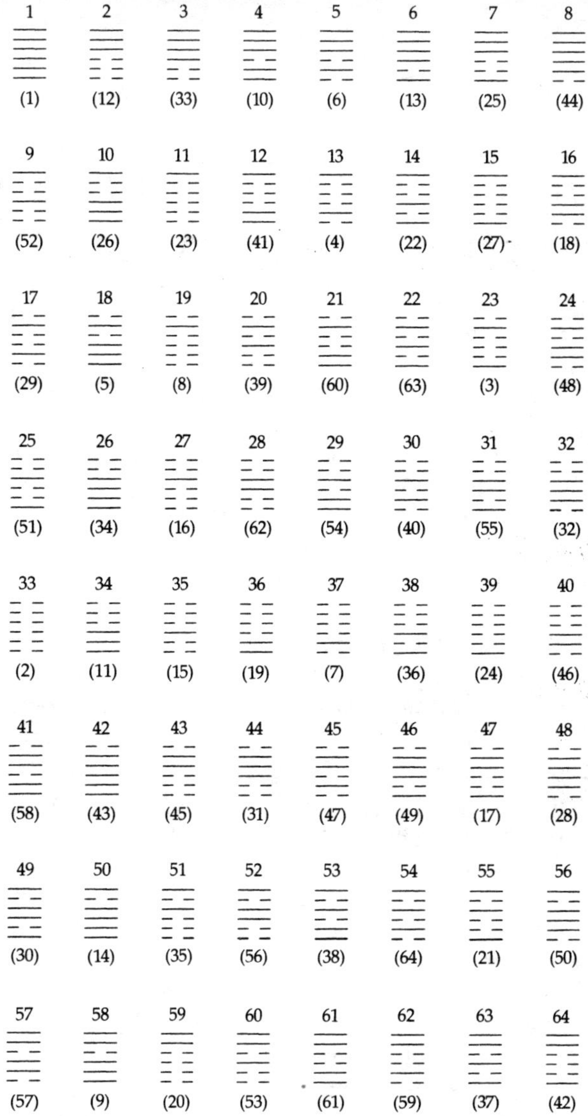

1	2	3	4	5	6	7	8
(1)	(12)	(33)	(10)	(6)	(13)	(25)	(44)

9	10	11	12	13	14	15	16
(52)	(26)	(23)	(41)	(4)	(22)	(27)	(18)

17	18	19	20	21	22	23	24
(29)	(5)	(8)	(39)	(60)	(63)	(3)	(48)

25	26	27	28	29	30	31	32
(51)	(34)	(16)	(62)	(54)	(40)	(55)	(32)

33	34	35	36	37	38	39	40
(2)	(11)	(15)	(19)	(7)	(36)	(24)	(46)

41	42	43	44	45	46	47	48
(58)	(43)	(45)	(31)	(47)	(49)	(17)	(28)

49	50	51	52	53	54	55	56
(30)	(14)	(35)	(56)	(38)	(64)	(21)	(50)

57	58	59	60	61	62	63	64
(57)	(9)	(20)	(53)	(61)	(59)	(37)	(42)

Figure 42
The sequence of the hexagrams from the Ma-wang-tui silk
manuscript. The numbers in brackets are those attributed to the
hexagrams in the standard modern editions.

2

The Current Sequence of the Hexagrams

At some point the original Ma-wang-tui sequence of the hexagrams, described in the previous appendix, dropped out of use and remained lost until its rediscovery in the twentieth century. This presumably occurred not long after 168 BC, and the sequence was replaced by the order of the hexagrams that we have today. The text was also divided into two 'books' of unequal length, with 30 hexagrams in the first book, and 34 in the second. The reason for this unequal division does not appear to have ever been satisfactorily explained. The same unequal format is also reflected in the *Hsü Kua Chuan*.

Whether the *Hsü Kua Chuan* was written contemporaneously with this revision is unclear. The explanations as to why and how the hexagrams succeed one another frequently appear to be forced, and the impression one gets on reading the commentary is that the author had no clear comprehension of the logic behind the sequence that he was trying to justify[1]. This may lead one to wonder whether there actually *is* any logic to the arrangement as it stands. Strangely, this question does not seem to have received any great attention either.

However, it is possible to find *some* evidence of structuring in the order of hexagrams as we have it today. This would appear to suggest that possibly the hexagrams were originally arranged in an order possessing a certain amount of logic and symmetry, but that this arrangement had already become corrupted by the time the *Hsü Kua Chuan* was written.

The modern order of the hexagrams is shown in Figure 43. As will be obvious to anyone acquainted with the *I Ching*, the hexagrams are arranged in pairs. Generally, the second hexagram

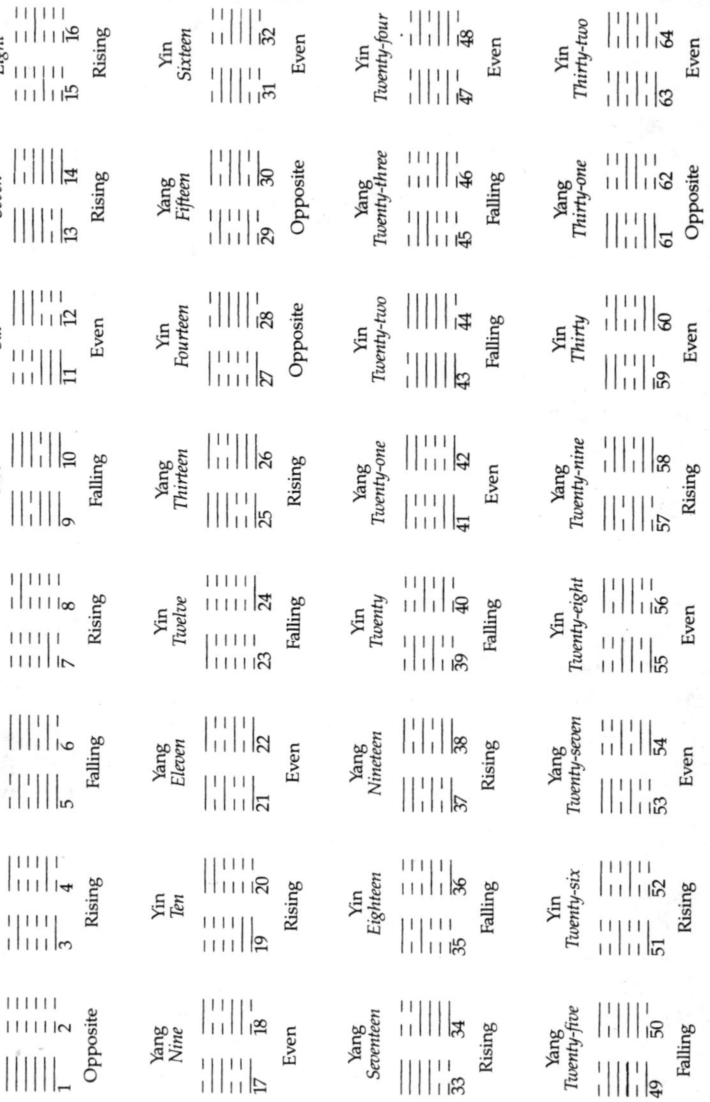

Figure 43
The Hexagram pairs. See accompanying text for explanation of terminology.

of each pair is the inverse of the first, as for example in the second pair, hexagrams 3 and 4. There are four exceptional pairs, where the hexagrams are opposite rather than inverse. These are the first pair, hexagrams 1 and 2; the fourteenth, hexagrams 27 and 28; the fifteenth, hexagrams 29 and 30; and the thirty-first, hexagrams 61 and 62. There are also, incidentally, four pairs where the hexagrams are both opposite and inverse: pairs six, nine, twenty-seven and thirty-two. However, being invertible, it appears that these pairs can be treated as if the opposition was unimportant.

Hexagrams 1 and 2, opposite in composition, make the first pair. Representing Heaven and Earth, the roots of all things, they are quite reasonably placed at the beginning of the book. With the succeeding pair positions, however, the first clues to the structure begin to appear. As pointed out in Chapter 1, odd numbers are treated as yang, even numbers as yin. The second pair position, being evenly numbered, would be designated yin. Here are to be found hexagrams 3 and 4, in which yin lines preponderate in each hexagram. The third pair position, designated yang, is occupied by hexagrams 5 and 6, in which yang lines preponderate in each hexagram. Generally speaking, where there is a preponderance of yang or yin lines in the hexagrams, this structure continues throughout the book. There is an exception, but we will return to this shortly. There are 10 pairs of hexagrams where there is an even split of three yang and three yin lines in each hexagram (pairs six, nine, eleven, sixteen, twenty-one, twenty-four, twenty- seven, twenty-eight, thirty, thirty-one). Six of these pairs fall in yin positions, four in yang. This uneven division may be further evidence of corruption. Also, there is no apparent reason why the majority of these 'even pairs' fall in the latter half of the book.

Returning to those pairs of hexagrams where either yang or yin preponderate, some further fragmentary evidence of structure may be found. Looking at Figure 43 again, let us concentrate on the second pair, with its preponderance of yin lines. In hexagram 3, the minority yang lines appear in line positions 1 and 5; in hexagram 4, the yang lines appear in positions 2 and 6. The minority lines can be said to rise upward from the first to the second hexagram of the pair. The opposite is the case in the third pair. In hexagram 5, the minority yin lines are placed in positions 4 and 6; in hexagram 6, they are placed in positions 1 and 3. The fourth pair shows a rise like the second, the fifth pair falls again. This rising and falling sequence reappears later, in pairs twelve and thirteen, pairs seventeen to twenty, and pairs twenty-five and twenty-six. This rising and falling sequence is, of course, frequently interrupted by even and opposite pairs. There are also exceptions. Pairs seven and eight are both 'rising'. This might seem to suggest that the hexagrams have been misplaced within the pairs; that hexagram 14 should come before 13, or alternatively, that 16 should come before 15. As we shall see, however, the problem is rather more complicated than this.

A similar argument could be made for pairs twenty-two and twenty-three, which are both 'falling'. Unfortunately though, something far worse has happened to these pairs. Pair twenty-two is a yin position, but is occupied by hexagrams 43 and 44, each of which contains five yang lines. Similarly, pair twenty-three falls in a yang position, but is occupied by hexagrams 45 and 46, each of which contain four yin lines. It would be easy to suggest a simple correction. Transpose the two pairs to bring them into the correct yang and yin positions, and then transpose the hexagrams in one pair to correct the rising-falling sequence. Again, however, this approach is rather too simplistic.

As Richard Wilhelm points out[2], the final hexagram in the *I Ching* as we have it today is number 64, Before Completion. This expresses the idea that, as one cycle of hexagrams comes to a close, so the way is left open for another to start. He goes on to say that the same idea is expressed in the *Tsa Kua Chuan* commentary (the 'Miscellaneous Notes'), where the final hexagram mentioned is number 43, Breakthrough. The logic of this is easy to see. In hexagram 43 five yang lines occupy the lower positions, about to 'rise up and push out' the yin line in the sixth place, and so return to the all-yang composition of hexagram 1, the Creative. Hexagram 43, it will be noted, falls in one of the 'misplaced' pairs.

If the *Tsa Kua Chuan* could be shown to be earlier than the *Hsü Kua Chuan*, we might look to it to provide an 'original' order of the hexagrams, which was then replaced by the order we have today. However, there is nothing to suggest that the *Tsa Kua Chuan* has any great priority; it appears to be roughly contemporary with the *Hsü Kua Chuan*. There is also no evidence to show that it contains an original ordered sequence that has since become corrupted. In fact, it contains even less logic in its arrangement than the order of the hexagrams in current editions of the *I Ching*.

If we consult the *Tsa Kua Chuan* as originally written[3] (rather than divided up by hexagrams as in Wilhelm's edition) we find that only 56 of the hexagrams are arranged in upright and inverse pairs. With the exception of the first pair, the pairs of hexagrams are treated in an order which bears no relation to that of the current edition; nor do the pairs show any sign of falling into numbered yang and yin positions. The last eight hexagrams treated by the commentary (in the current edition numbered 28, 44, 53, 27, 63, 54, 64, 43) are not paired, and are curiously jumbled. At first sight then, the *Tsa Kua Chuan* appears to offer no help.

Nonetheless, by putting all the evidence together, it is possible to make some tentative speculations about the original structure of the current order. The first step would be to note an almost compulsive Chinese desire for symmetry, especially in matters such as the balanced principles of yang and yin. From this, it might appear logical to propose that the original structure consisted of two equal halves, with 32 hexagrams in each half, rather than the current divisions of 30 and 34 hexagrams.

The next step is to examine the positioning of the opposite pairs of hexagrams (1,2; 27,28; 29,30; 61,62). These currently fall in pair positions one, fourteen, fifteen and thirty-one. These pairs would more logically fall at positions one, sixteen, seventeen and thirty-two, with a central division of the book into two equal halves. In this case, the first book would open with the major embodiments of yang and yin, The Creative and The Receptive, Heaven and Earth. It would finish with Corners of the Mouth and Preponderance of the Great. The second book would also open with major embodiments of yang and yin, but here symmetrically reversed so that yin comes before yang. These are The Abysmal, the moon and water; and The Clinging, the sun and fire. The second book would end with Inner Truth and Preponderance of the Small, which are structurally very similar to Corners of the Mouth and Preponderance of the Great. This would be symmetrically very satisfying.

However, if the emphasis of the interpretation was then to be changed, so that symmetry came to be less important than the concept of a continuous cycle, there might be cause to rearrange the sequence. Although the *Hsü Kua Chuan* says that Preponderance of the Small 'signifies a transition', its symmetrically balanced structure might seem less aesthetically satisfying than, for instance, one of the more 'progressive' hexagrams like Breakthrough or Before Completion.

It is necessary to conjecture two stages of revision, both of them carried out by persons either prepared to disregard the intrinsic symmetry of the original arrangement in favour of a cyclical interpretation, or unaware of it. In the first stage, we can suppose that Breakthrough (along with its attendant pairing, Coming to Meet) was moved from another position to the end of the book. At this stage, the pair would appear in reverse positions to that which they do today; Coming to Meet would be followed by Breakthrough. It might be supposed that this was the original order, and that they were only reversed when the pair was moved again to its current position; in due course we shall see some slight evidence that this is not the case.

The result of this first transposition would be that all the pairs following after the original position of Breakthrough and Coming to Meet would be moved back one pair position in the order. Let us further suppose that the Breakthrough pair were originally moved from the first half of the book. This would then have several consequences.

First, all the pairings subsequent to the original position of the Breakthrough pair would have moved into incorrect yang and yin pair positions. Second, the last opposite pair (Inner Truth and Preponderance of the Small) would move back to pair position thirty-one, where they remain today. Third, the two central opposite pairs (Corners of the Mouth and Preponderance of the Great; The Abysmal and The Clinging) would be pushed back from pair positions sixteen and seventeen to fifteen and sixteen. We can suppose that the division of the book into two parts would have remained, at this stage, between the two opposite pairs. This would give two unequal parts of 30 and 34 hexagrams respectively; the same format as appears today, but with Preponderance of the Great being hexagram 30.

The *Tsa Kua Chuan* may date from this stage of revision. The original logical and symmetrical arrangement of the *I Ching* having been destroyed, the author of this commentary may have felt himself free to deal with its hexagrams in any order he chose, with the exception of acknowledging that the book began with The Creative, and ended with Breakthrough.

However, it must next be supposed that for some reason Breakthrough was then also thought to make an unsatisfactory ending. In the second stage of revision, this was replaced by Before Completion (again with its attendant pairing, After Completion). This time, though, the revision is not so simple.

The Completion pair would again appear to have been brought from the first half of the book. The removal of a second pair from the first part would generally have brought the remaining pairs throughout the rest of the book back to their correct yang and yin positions. This would be especially true if this pair was originally placed next to the Breakthrough pair. This seems quite possible, simply on the grounds that such a position does least violence to the order.

Can we make any conjecture as to where these two pairs were originally placed? One possibility suggests itself from the peculiarity about pairs seven and eight already mentioned. These are both 'rising' pairs. Instead of reversing the hexagrams in one pair to bring them back into a rising-falling sequence, it might be suggested that the two removed pairs should be placed between pairs seven and eight. The Completion pair are 'even', with equal numbers of yang and yin lines in each hexagram. These would be placed in yin pair-position eight, following the rising pair seven. Breakthrough and Coming to Meet are a yang pair, and would thus fit into yang pair position nine. If they were originally in this order, Breakthrough appearing first, they would be a 'falling' pair, which would then be followed by the rising pair of hexagrams 15 and 16. This would then restore the rising-falling sequence for this section of the book. The reconstruction of this section would thus run hexagrams 1–14, 63, 64, 43, 44, 15 and onwards.

However, is there any good reason to designate the Breakthrough pair as 'falling'? There are four opposite and 10 even pairs, leaving 18 pairs to be divided into rising and falling. That some sort of fairly symmetrical rising-falling sequence is being sought would seem to be suggested by the solid groupings of hexagrams 3 to 10 and 33 to 40. At first sight, it would seem that the most logical method would be to have nine rising and nine falling pairs, and then to distribute them evenly between the two halves of the book; but this is not possible. To split nine rising pairs into two halves would fit four-and-a-half pairs into each book; likewise with the nine falling pairs. To have nine rising and nine falling pairs would require an assymetrical distribution between the two halves of the book. In the current sequence there are, however, 10 rising pairs and eight falling pairs. It is still possible to maintain an alternation of rising and falling pairs with these numbers by both starting and finishing the sequence in the first half with rising pairs, and by doing the same with the sequence in the second half. However, this can only be achieved if the Breakthrough pair is included among the total of eight falling pairs. If it were a rising pair, Coming to Meet followed by Breakthrough, there would be 11 rising pairs and seven falling, which would make it impossible to maintain the continuous alternation. This would seem to argue that in the original structure Breakthrough was followed by Coming to Meet, as they stand today . . . a falling pair.

As a result of removing a second pair of hexagrams from the first half of the book during the second revision, the two central opposite pairs moved back to their current positions as pairs fourteen and fifteen. However, this time the division of the book (after 30 hexagrams) does not appear to have moved with them. Thus both these central opposite pairs appear at the end of the first book, rather than split between the first and second parts.

At the first stage of revision, it was conjectured that *all* the pairs were moved back one place after the removal of the Breakthrough pair. This does not seem to have been the case in the second revision. The Completion pair was brought from the first half of the book and placed at the end of the entire sequence. Rather than moving the Breakthrough pair back from position thirty-two to thirty-one (and likewise those pairs immediately prior to it), the pair was instead dislodged to an entirely different position. It appears in the current edition at pair position twenty-two, between the even pair of hexagrams 41 and 42, and the yin pair of 45 and 46. This placed the yang Breakthrough pair in a yin position, and also pushed the yin pair of hexagrams 45 and 46 into a yang position.

Nonetheless, when the Breakthrough pair occupied pair position thirty-two, they would have been in the reversed order, Coming to Meet being placed first. They have been switched round once again in the move to their position in the current order. The only reasoning for this forced positional fit and further reversal would seem to come from the *Hsü Kua Chuan*. There we find that an 'Increase' (42) is said to be certainly followed by a 'Breakthrough' (43); such resoluteness leads to 'Coming to Meet' (44), and this is followed

by 'Gathering Together' (45). There is a certain logic here, if perhaps
a little forced. It might be conjectured that the *Hsü Kua Chuan* is
contemporaneous with this second stage of revision, and was
written to justify the revised order; it can obviously be no earlier.

This is really as far as it is safe to go on the evidence. There are
still problems, but any further reconstruction of an original order
involves so many variables that it cannot be attempted, or even
guessed, with any confidence. To carry through such a
reconstruction in full would result in a sequence barely recognizable
by comparison with the one we have today.

The first problem comes about when the Breakthrough pair is
removed from the second half of the book and placed in the first.
The yin pair of hexagrams 45 and 46 can then be moved back one
place from their current yang position to occupy a yin one. However,
it is not possible to simply move the following pairs back one place
in turn for the whole of the rest of the sequence. The pairs would
then fall in wrong yang and yin positions. The remaining
hexagrams after 46 have to be juggled quite violently to bring them
into the right positions.

The next problem is that even if the Breakthrough and
Completion pairs are moved to the first half of the book, there
still remains a sequence that runs through hexagrams 15 and 16
(rising), 17 and 18 (even) and 19 and 20 (rising). Similarly, in the
second half there would be a sequence of hexagrams 39, 40 (falling),
41, 42 (even) and 45, 46 (falling). It would be easy to transpose one
of the rising pairs in the first half with one of the falling pairs in
the second; but there is still a further problem. There are still only
four even pairs in the first half of the book, and six in the
second. A better solution might be to transpose one of the even
pairs in the second half with one of the rising pairs in the first,
and then to further alter the order in the second half to maintain
a correct alternation of rising and falling.

One such possible reconstruction is offered in Figure 44. It shows
an order in which the book is divided into two equal halves, each
beginning and ending with an opposite pair. The even pairs are
arranged five to each half and equally split so that five fall in yang
positions, five in yin. Also, it maintains a strict alternation of rising
and falling within each half, even where the pairs are divided from
one another by intervening even pairs. However, this sequence is
offered with the greatest hesitation. The violence it does to the

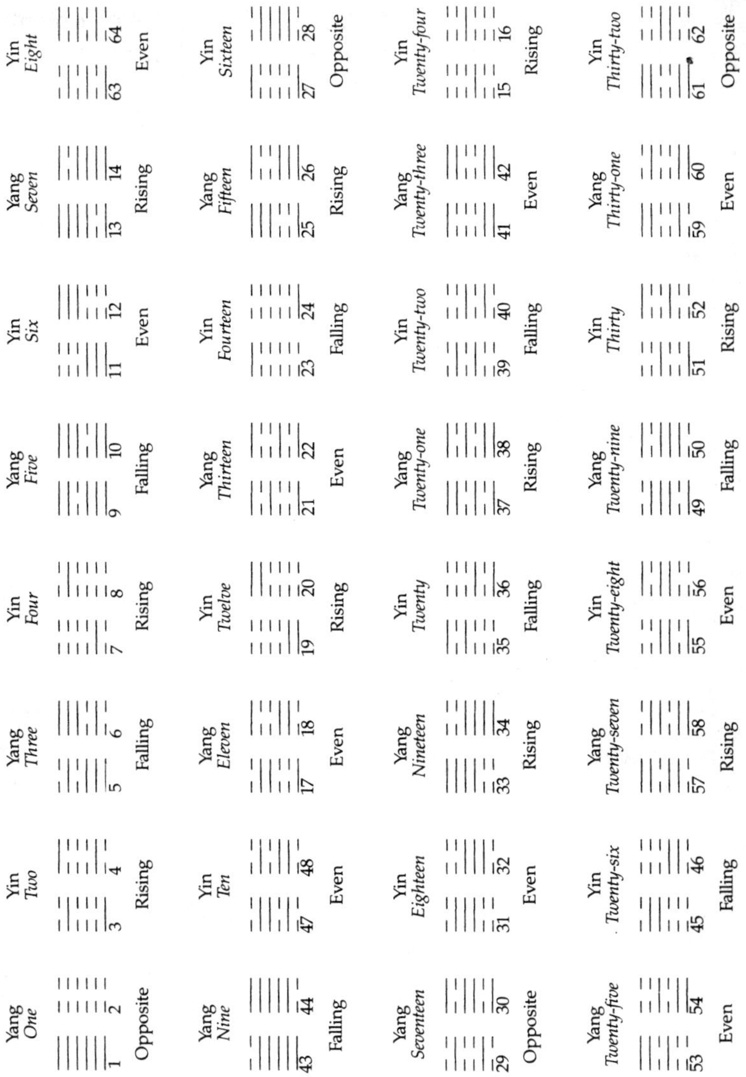

Figure 44
One possible reconstruction of the original order of the hexagrams. See accompanying text for explanation.

current order is glaringly obvious, and the arrangement is constructed entirely on the basis of bringing the sequence into a more logical and symmetrical form. It is also only one of many such possible reconstructions; there are too many variables involved to place all the hexagrams with certainty.

The conclusions drawn here naturally have to remain no more than tentative. Nonetheless, there does seem to be some evidence of an original and more symmetrical structure, and of its later corruption. What that original structure was will have to remain no more than speculation . . . unless, perhaps, another chance archaeological find, like the Ma-wang-tui manuscript, settles the question once and for all.

3
The Worship of T'ai I and the Paces of Yü

The magic square of three, and the magic line by which its positions are read in numerical order, can be dated at least as early as the Han dynasty. One example of its use appears in the official Han religion, in the worship of T'ai I, 'The Great Unity'. T'ai I is mentioned in literature as early as the fourth century BC, and his worship may date back to the same period. However, his elevation to a position in Imperial cult can be dated quite precisely to 123 BC, during the reign of the Han emperor Wu Ti, who seems to have especially favoured the deity[1].

The abode of T'ai I was at the (Northern) celestial pole. There does, however, seem to be considerable confusion in Chinese texts between the actual celestial pole and the constellation of the Dipper (the seven major stars of Ursa Major); either name is used interchangeably for the axis of the heavens. Indeed, the Dipper is sometimes referred to in Han texts as 'T'ai I's chariot' (the four stars making the 'bowl' of the Dipper) and 'T'ai I's spear' (the three stars of the 'handle')[2].

T'ai I dwelt in the 'Nine Palaces'. These consisted of a central palace surrounded by eight others which correlated with the eight directions and the eight trigrams in the World of the Senses arrangement. He was said to circulate through these Nine Palaces during the course of a year[3]. That these palaces were also correlated with the magic square of three can be gathered from various early texts. The *Ch'ien Tso Tu*, one of the apocryphal *I Wei* texts, says:

> The yang in operating advances, changing from 7 to 9 and thus symbolizing the waxing of its ether. The yin in operating withdraws, changing from 8 to 6 and thus symbolizing the waning of its ether.

Therefore the Supreme One (T'ai I) takes these (yin and yang) numbers as it circulates among the nine halls, (which include) the four main compass points and the four intermediary compass points. (The numbers of the trigrams) in every case add up to 15. [4]

The numbers 6, 7, 8 and 9 obviously refer to the numbers of the yin and yang lines in the *I Ching*. The passage of interest here is that which refers to the numbers 'in every case adding up to 15'. The numbers of the magic square of three add up to 15 in every direction, horizontally, vertically and diagonally. It might be argued that the text refers instead to the numbers of the yang and yin (7 + 8 = 15, 9 + 6 = 15). However, it is the number of the trigrams, the eight numbers arranged around the centre, which are said to add up to 15. Further confirmation that the reference is to the magic square of three comes from the actual path followed by the deity during the year.

T'ai I's circulation among the nine heavenly palaces is described in terms of the trigrams and the directions. First, he travels North (K'an); second, South-West (K'un); third, East (Chên); fourth, South-East (Sun) and fifthly back to the Centre to rest. Then, sixthly, he travels North-West (Ch'ien); seventh, West (Tui); eighth, North-East (Kên); and ninth, South (Li). Reference to the Lo Shu diagram in Chapter 4 (Figure 6) will show that in travelling such a course T'ai I was following the magic line of three [5]. T'ai I was worshipped on an octagonal altar with eight 'spirit paths' marked on it. Whether the ritual involved the worshipper in any form of motion that followed the same magic line is not known [6].

T'ai I's nine celestial palaces were said to correspond to the nine provinces of China in the world below. His worship did not survive the period of disunity which followed the fall of the Han dynasty, although the magic line of three did. It is not surprising to find that the form in which it continued was transferred to the earthly realm, and to those same nine provinces. It was known in later times as the 'Paces of Yü', and was said to represent the course which the legendary Emperor Yü followed while travelling through the provinces to quell the Chinese great flood. One of the reasons for this attribution may be that the Lo Shu and Ho T'u diagrams were originally supposed to have been given to Yü to assist him in his task [7].

However, the earliest existing description of something called

'The Paces of Yü' does not refer to the magic square or its line, although it is directly related to the Dipper. The description dates from about AD 320, and is given by the writer Ko Hung as follows[8]:

> Advance left foot, then pass it with the right. Bring the left up to the right foot. Advance right foot, then pass it with the left. Bring the right up to the left foot. Advance left foot, then pass it with the right. Bring the left up to the right foot. In this way three paces are made, a total of 21 linear feet, and nine footprints will be made.

This method of pacing appears to have been used largely as a measure for ritual protection, or for aligning oneself with the correct stellar influences. It is said by Ko Hung to be employed in a variety of instances: in gathering alchemical minerals, in avoiding plague, or in approaching ghost-infested mountains and forests[9].

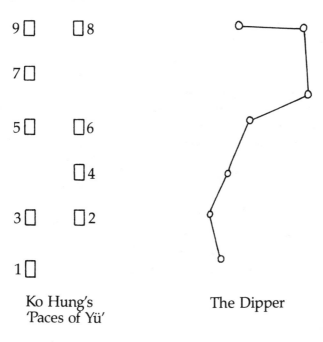

Ko Hung's   The Dipper
'Paces of Yü'

Figure 45

These paces are said to represent the stars of the Dipper[10] and, from Figure 45, it can be seen that the pattern trodden is similar.

The pattern is, however, reversed, like a mirror-image. The only logical reason for this would appear to be that the constellation of the Dipper as seen in the sky is looked at from below. When the Dipper is brought down on to the ground, it is seen from above. It is thus looked at 'from the other side', in a reversed form.

The problem with the Dipper, of course, is that it only has seven stars, and seven was not a particularly significant number in Chinese thinking. Thus in later Taoist thought two 'invisible stars' are added to it to bring the number up to nine[11]. There may be a forerunner to this addition in Ko Hung's pacing, where nine footsteps are used to represent the pattern of the seven-starred constellation. This nine-starred Dipper has become well established even in popular iconography. A Chinese ring in the author's possession shows the Dipper with nine stars; the star lying at each end of the constellation is shown in double form.

The addition of the two extra stars probably reflects a desire to correlate the constellation more fully with the nine halls of T'ai I's palace in the heavens. The result is that the physical constellation is quite forgotten and replaced with nine 'stars' shuffled together into the pattern of the magic square. This allows the nine paces of Ko Hung's version, with its association with the Dipper, to be brought into line with the Lo Shu magic square and the course of Yü's travels through the provinces.

The Paces of Yü are used in many Taoist rituals to this day, and a number of these are discussed in Chapter 9. Additional mention might be made here of the P'u-tu ritual. Having originated in heaven with the circulation of T'ai I and descended to earth with the Paces of Yü, the magic line here makes its final appearance in the underworld. In this ritual the nine courts of punishment in the Chinese hell are believed to be arranged in the Lo Shu magic square. The Taoist gathers the tormented souls together and leads them through the nine courts according to the Paces of Yü, before delivering them to the tenth court for their final release[12].

References

Only brief citations by author's name and page number are given here. For full title, date and publication details, see Bibliography.

Chapter 1

1. Wilhelm/Baynes: passim.
2. Blofeld: passim.
3. Legge (3): passim.
4. Whincup: passim.
5. Needham: vol 2, 273–274.
6. Henderson: 170.
7. Loewe (2): 26–27.
8. Swanson (2): 71.
9. Wilhelm/Baynes: 262–279.
10. Needham: vol 3, 625. Ritsema: 187.
11. Wilhelm, Hellmut (2): 115.
12. Henderson: 7.
13. Needham: vol 2, 253–261.
14. Fort: 544.
15. Needham: vol 3, 507–508.
16. De Bary: vol 1, 199.
17. Loewe (2): 42.
18. Needham: vol 2, 357-358.
19. De Bary: vol 1, 205.

Chapter 2

1. Watson (1): vol 2, 472.

2. Wilhelm/Baynes: lviii-lix.
3. Swanson (1): 104–105.
4. Waley: 123.
5. Wilhelm, Hellmut (2): 52–89.
6. Shchutskii: 136ff. Swanson (1): 105.
7. Chen, Shih-chuan: 237.
8. Waley: 138. Wilhelm, Hellmut (2): 56.
9. Whincup: passim. Wilhelm, Hellmut (2): 52–64.
10. Shchutskii: 194.
11. Shchutskii: 194.
12. Shchutskii: 194. Wilhelm, Hellmut (2): 64–69.
13. Needham: vol 2, 350.
14. Needham: vol 2, 307, 350.
15. Needham: vol 2, 391.
16. Chen, Shih-chuan: 239.
17. Chen, Shih-chuan: 247.
18. Anon (2): 22. Ho: 32. Loewe & Blacker: 61. *Wen Wu*: 1974, No 7, col. plate 1. *Wen Wu*: 1974, No 9, 45–57. Xiong: 31.
19. *Wen Wu*: 1974, No 9, 53.
20. Whincup: passim.
21. *Wen Wu*: 1974, No 9, 48.
22. Wilhelm/Baynes: lviii.
23. Maspero: 233–234.
24. Chen, Shih-chuan: 238. Shchutskii: 81, 95–98.
25. Maspero: 233.
26. Needham: vol 2, 343. Wilhelm, Hellmut (2): 34.
27. Waley: 127.
28. Needham: vol 2, 343. vol 3, 6–7.
29. Needham: vol 3, 4.
30. Needham: vol 2, 343.
31. Wilhelm, Hellmut (1): 90–91.
32. Sung: 135–138. Wilhelm/Baynes: 542–545.
33. Sung: 219–222. Wilhelm/Baynes: 654–656.
34. Sung: 155–158.
35. Waley: 127.
36. Sung: 31–34.
37. Loewe (2): 182. Loewe & Blacker: 48.
38. Hooke: 317.
39. San: 14–26, 27–40.
40. Moore: passim. Needham: vol 2, 248.

41. Henderson: 33–35. Needham: vol 2, 232–241. Yang & Yang: 71–72.
42. Louton: 106–107.
43. Loewe (2): 153.
44. Loewe (2): 41.
45. Hart: 61.
46. Waltham/Legge: 125–132.
47. Needham: vol 2, 242.
48. *Analects*: 7; 20. Legge (2): 201.
49. Wilhelm/Baynes: 529.
50. *Analects*: 7; 16. Legge (2): 200.
51. Shchutskii: 116, 124.
52. Needham: vol 2, 274.
53. Henderson: 184.
54. Needham: vol 2, 274.
55. Shchutskii: 105.
56. Shchutskii: 159–161.
57. *Wen Wu*: 1974, No 9, 40.
58. Needham: vol 2, 307 (except dates of *Shuo Kua Chuan*: see notes 56, 57).
59. Bruce: passim.

Chapter 3

1.   Swanson (2): 77–79.
2.   Needham: vol 2, 258.
3.   Cammann (2): 46–50.
4.   Major: 146–149.
5.   De Bary: vol 1, 199. Forke: 240–241.
6.   Moore: passim.
7.   Chan: 282. Hart: 61.
8.   Chan: 282–283. Fung: vol 2, 56. Needham: vol 2, 279–291. vol 5, pt 4, 308–309.
9.   Jung: passim.
10. Hu Shih: 37.
11. Hu Shih: 34–38. Moore: passim. Tjan: 241–3, 489–492.
12. Needham: vol 2, 287.
13. Tjan: 49.
14. Cammann (1): 200.
15. Cahill: 310.

16.   Henderson: 81.
17.   Cammann (2): 72. Needham: vol 4, pt 1, 271–272.
18.   Tjan: 405–409, 534, 566.
19.   Tjan: 233.
20.   Saso (1): 135.

Chapter 4

1.   Needham: vol 4, pt 1, 296.
2.   Loewe (1): 205.
3.   Needham: vol 4, pt 1, 296–297. De Woskin: 118.
4.   Bruce: 104, 106.
5.   Wilhelm/Baynes: 268.
6.   Wilhelm/Baynes: 268–270.
7.   Fung: vol 2, 102–103.
8.   Blofeld: 218.
9.   Saso (2): 404.
10.   Needham: vol 3, 56.
11.   Bruce: 106. Fung: vol 2, 101.
12.   Cammann (2): 39. Fung: vol 2, 146. Henderson: 86.
      Needham: vol 2, 393.
13.   Major: 146–150.
14.   Wilhelm/Baynes: 308.
15.   Waltham/Legge: 126.
16.   Forke: 284–285. Fung: vol 2, 14.
17.   Shchutskii: 76.
18.   Waltham/Legge: 39–54.
19.   Pang: 112–113. Saso (1): 136–140, 264–265.
20.   Cammann (2): 51.
21.   Loewe (1): 112–115.
22.   Loewe (1): 125–126.
23.   Soymie: 285.
24.   Loewe (1): 41.
25.   Schafer (2): 105.
26.   Loewe (1): 86–126.
27.   Cahill: 6–142.
28.   Cahill: 6–8.
29.   *Chuang Tzu*: 6; 7. Legge (1): vol 1, 245.
30.   Cahill: 9.
31.   Loewe (2): 214.

32. Loewe (1): 90.
33. Soymie: 285–286.
34. Cahill: 17-18. Werner (2): 163-164.
35. Watson (1): vol 2, 472.
36. Schafer (2): 52.
37. Watson (1): vol 2, 268.
38. Loewe (1): 97.
39. Loewe (1): 98–101. Loewe (2): 120.
40. Cahill: passim.
41. Le Blanc: 170.
42. Bodde (1): 386–389. Fung: vol 1, 397. Soymie: 276–277.
    Werner (2): 334–335.
43. Bodde (1): 386–389. Soymie: 286. Werner (2): 334–335.
44. Soymie: 277–280.
45. Maspero: 356. Werner (2): 234.
46. Werner (2): 163, 234.
47. Watson (1): vol 2, 289.
48. Werner (2): 163.
49. Waltham/Legge: 19.
50. Soymie: 278–279. Werner (2): 159.
51. Werner (2): 43, 159, 163–164, 418–419, 594.
52. Soymie: 284. Werner (2): 163–164, 234.
53. Ch'ên Mêng-lei: vol 4, 1286.
54. Wilhelm/Baynes: 279.
55. Loewe (1): 34, 38.
56. Needham: vol 2, 311.
57. Wilhelm/Baynes: 273, 276.
58. Wilhelm/Baynes: 273.
59. Werner (1): 186–187.
60. Wilhelm/Baynes: 587.
61. Wilhelm/Baynes: 273.

Chapter 5

1. *Wen Wu*: 1974, No 9, 40.
2. Wilhelm/Baynes: 265.
3. Fung: vol 2, 440.
4. Fung: vol 2, 459–461.
5. Chen, Shih-chuan: 239–241.
6. Wilhelm/Baynes: 264.

7.   Liu Ts'un-yan: 300.
8.   Fung: vol 2, 426–430. Liu Ts'un-yan: 302–303. Needham: vol 5, pt 3, 62–66. Wu & Davis: 234–235.
9.   Fung: vol 2, 430. Wu & Davis: 235.
10. Liu Ts'un-yan: 302–303.
11. Needham: vol 2, 442.
12. *I Ching Chên Ch'uan*: T'u Shuo, Fol. 1b.
13. Cammann (2): 58.
14. Saso (2): 399–416.
15. Needham: vol 3, 59.
16. Major: 150–152.
17. Saso (2): 402.
18. Saso (2): 401–403.
19. *I Ching Chên Ch'uan*: T'u Shuo, Fol. 3a.
20. Needham: vol 3, 625. Ritsema: 187. Wilhelm, Hellmut (2): 115.

Chapter 6

1.   Blofeld: 218.
2.   *I Ching Chên Ch'uan*: T'u Shuo, Fol 2a.

Chapter 7

1.   Loewe (1): 125–126. Werner (2): 594.
2.   Bodde (1): 387. Loewe (1): 4, 74, 77, 79. Needham: vol 3, 214. Soymie: 276.

Chapter 8

1.   Li Shu Hua: 84–85. Loewe (1): 75–80, 204–208. Needham: vol 4, pt 1, 261–269.
2.   Needham: vol 4, pt 1: 240.
3.   Eitel: passim. Feuchtwang: passim. De Groot: vol 3, 935–1055. Lip: passim. Needham: vol 4, pt 1, 293–313. Skinner: passim.
4.   Ch'ên Ying Lüeh: see bibliography for full list of titles.
5.   Needham: vol 2, 206.
6.   Liu, Da: 44–45. Lu Hsun: 78–79.
7.   Werner (2): 232–233.

8. Dennys: 134–135.
9. Griffith: 160. Williams: 189–190.
10. Werner (2): 177, 515.
11. Anon (1) : plate 109.
12. Williams: 391.

Chapter 9

1. Brewitt-Taylor: vol 2. 421–422.
2. See note 4 to Chapter 8.
3. Li/Hsu: 102
4. Watson (1): vol 2, 472.
5. *San Kuo Chih*: vol 1, 47.
6. Bodde (2): 331.
7. De Crespigny (2): 45.
8. Bodde (2): 328.
9. Griffith: passim.
10. Bodde (2): 331.
11. Bodde (2): 331.
12. Knechtges: 17–18.
13. I shall cover this material more fully in a forthcoming paper for *Fortean Times*.
14. Tan Manni: 41.
15. Kermadec: 7.
16. Palmer: 142–149. Full text in most Chinese almanacs.
17. *Chu-ko Liang Chi*: passim.
18. Leban: 344.
19. De Crespigny (1): 14. *San Kuo Chih*: passim.
20. *Chu-ko Liang Chi*: xx. *San Kuo Chih*: vol 4, 927 (trans: author).
21. *Chu-ko Liang Chi*: xxi. *San Kuo Chih*: vol 4, 929.
22. De Crespigny (1): 12.
23. Yao: xxix.
24. *Chu-ko Liang Chi*: xxii-xxiii. *San Kuo Chih*: vol 4, 929.
25. *Chu-ko Liang Chi*: 44 (trans: author).
26. Yao: xxix (trans: author).
27. Tang Zhongpu: 49.
28. Yao: xxix (trans: author).
29. Ho: 34.
30. Cooper: 226.

31.　　Hsia: 332.
32.　　Brewitt-Taylor: vol 2, 251-253. Lo Kuan-chung: vol 2, 673–674.
33.　　Fang: vol 1, 91–134.
34.　　Brewitt-Taylor: vol 2, 423–424. Lo Kuan-chung: vol 2, 811–812.
35.　　Brewitt-Taylor: vol 2, 552–553. Lo Kuan-chung: vol 2, 911–913.
36.　　Watson (2): 107–108. Legge (1): vol 1, 388–389.
37.　　Cammann (2): 74.
38.　　Chu & Sherrill: 11, 440. Sherrill & Chu: 76–82.
39.　　Ho: 34.
40.　　Loewe (1): 204–208.
41.　　Cahill: 106.
42.　　Hou, Ching-lang: 210–211.
43.　　*Ju-lai Shên-chang*: 96 (10 Dec 83), 27. 98 (24 Dec 83), 29.
44.　　Yang & Yang: 238–252.
45.　　Huang Pên-ying: 237–126.
46.　　Saso (1): 138–139.
47.　　Saso (1): 17–18, 129–130.
48.　　Saso (1): 127–192.
49.　　Saso (1): 223.
50.　　Saso (1): 244–246.
51.　　Saso (1): 260–261.

Appendix 1

1.　　*Wen Wu*: 1974. No 9, 48.

Appendix 2

1.　　Lee: 6. Legge (3): 54–55.
2.　　Wilhelm/Baynes: 718.
3.　　Sung: 366–369.

Appendix 3

1.　　Fung: vol 2, 101.
2.　　Cammann (2): 61, 71.
3.　　Cammann (2): 63.

4. Fung: vol 2, 101.
5. Cammann (2): 63–64.
6. Fung: vol 2, 101. Watson (1): vol 2, 40.
7. Needham: vol 3, 57.
8. Ware: 198.
9. Ware: 180, 260, 285.
10. Schafer (1): 239.
11. Schafer (1): 239–240.
12. Pang: 112–113.

Bibliography

Analects: see Legge (2).

Anon, *Historical Relics Unearthed in New China*, Foreign Languages Press, Peking, 1972.

Anon, 'More Cultural Relics Found in Ancient Mawangdui Tombs', *Peking Review*, Vol 17, No 35, 22–23. Peking, 30 Aug. 1974.

De Bary, William Theodore, *Sources of Chinese Tradition*, 2 vols, Columbia University Press, New York & London, 1960.

Le Blanc, Charles, *Huai Nan Tzu: Philosophical Synthesis in Early Han Thought*, Hong Kong University Press, Hong Kong, 1985.

Blofeld, John, *I Ching*, George Allen & Unwin, London, 1965.

Bodde, Derk, 'Myths of Ancient China', in Samuel Noah Kramer (ed) *Mythologies of the Ancient World*, 367–408, Doubleday, New York, 1961.

——, *Festivals in Classical China*, Princeton University Press, New Jersey, 1975.

Brewitt-Taylor, C.H., *The Romance of the Three Kingdoms*, 2 vols, (1925), Charles E Tuttle, Vermont & Tokyo, 1959.

Bruce, Percy, 'The *I Wei*, a Problem in Criticism'. *Journal of the Royal Asiatic Society, North China Branch*, Vol 61, 100–107, Shanghai, 1930.

Cahill, Suzanne Elizabeth, *The Image of the Goddess Hsi Wang Mu in Medieval Chinese Literature*. Unpublished Ph.D. dissertation, University of California, 1982.

Cammann, Schuyler, 'Types of Symbols in Chinese Art', in Arthur F. Wright (ed) *Studies in Chinese Thought*, 195–231, Chicago University Press, 1953.

——, 'The Magic Square of Three in Old Chinese Philosophy and Religion', *History of Religions*, Vol 1, No 1, 37–80, Chicago, 1961.

Chan, Wing-Tsit, *A Sourcebook in Chinese Philosophy*, Princeton University Press, New Jersey, 1963.

Ch'ên Mêng-Lei, *Chou-I Ch'ien-Shu*, 4 vols, (1694, in Chinese), Shanghai Ku Chi Ch'u Pan Shê, Shanghai, 1983.

Chen, Shih-Chuan, 'How to Form a Hexagram and Consult the I Ching'. *Journal of the American Oriental Society*, Vol 92, No 2, 237–249, Baltimore, April–June 1972.

Ch'ên Ying Lüeh, The 'Kuei Ku Tzŭ Books' (in Chinese). *Kuei Ku Tzŭ tou chih chüeh chi* (Kuei Ku Tzŭ's extraordinary arts in the struggle for wisdom), *Kuei Ku Tzŭ shên chi ping fa* (Kuei Ku Tzŭ's occult military strategy), *Kuei Ku Tzŭ wu tzu t'ien shu* (Kuei Ku Tzŭ's secret book of heaven), *Kuei Ku Tzŭ chih hsiao jên shu* (Kuei Ku Tzŭ's art of governing inferior men), *Kuei Ku Tzŭ tsung hêng tou chih shu* (Kuei Ku Tzŭ's length and breadth of the struggle for wisdom), *Kuei Ku Tzŭ san liu wu ti shên chao* (Kuei Ku Tzŭ's 36 matchless spirit invocations), Hsin Li Shu Chu, Hong Kong, n.d.

Chu, W.K., & Sherrill, W.A., *The Astrology of the I Ching*, Routledge & Kegan Paul, London, 1976.

Chuang Tzŭ: see Legge, Watson.

Chu-ko Liang Chi, (In Chinese), Chung Hua Shu Chu, Peking, 1960.

Cooper, Arthur, *Li Po and Tu Fu*, Penguin Books, Harmondsworth, 1973.

Creel, H.G., *Confucius and the Chinese Way*, Harper, New York, 1960.

De Crespigny, Rafe, *The Records of the Three Kingdoms*, Australian National University, Centre of Oriental Studies, Occasional Paper No 9, Canberra, 1970.

——, *Northern Frontier, The Policies and Strategy of the Later Han Empire*, Faculty of Asian Studies Monographs, New Series No 4, Australian National University, Canberra, 1984.

Dennys, Nicholas B., *The Folklore of China*, (1876), Oriental Press, Amsterdam, 1968.

Eitel, E.J., *Feng Shui*, (1873), Cokaygne, Cambridge, 1973.

Fang, Achilles, *The Chronicle of the Three Kingdoms*, 2 vols, Harvard-Yenching Institute Studies VI, Harvard University Press, Massachusetts, 1952, 1965.

Feuchtwang, Stephan D.R., *An Anthropological Analysis of Chinese Geomancy*, Vithagna, Vientiane, Laos, 1974.

Forke, Alfred, *The World Conception of the Chinese*, (1925), Arno Press, New York, 1975.

Fort, Charles, *The Complete Books of Charles Fort*, (1941), Dover Books, New York, 1974.

Fung, Yu-lan, *A History of Chinese Philosophy*, 2 vols, Princeton University Press, New Jersey, 1952.

Griffith, Samuel B., *Sun Tzu, The Art of War*, Oxford University Press, 1963.

De Groot, J.J.M., *The Religious System of China*, 6 vols, (1892–1912), Literature House, Taiwan, 1964.

Hart, James A., 'The Speech of Prince Chin: A study of Early Chinese Cosmology', In Henry Rosemont Jr (ed), *Explorations in Chinese Cosmology*, 35–66, JAAR Thematic Studies 50/2, Scholars Press, Chico, California, 1984.

Henderson, John B., *The Development and Decline of Chinese Cosmology*, Columbia University Press, New York, 1984.

Ho Peng Yoke, 'The Book of Changes and Traditional Chinese Science', *New Horizon*, Vol 18, No 12, 31–37, Hong Kong, December, 1979.

Hook, Brian (ed), *The Cambridge Encyclopedia of China*, Cambridge University Press, 1982.

Hou, Ching-lang: 'The Chinese Belief in Baleful Stars', In Holmes Welch & Anna Seidel (eds), *Facets of Taoism*, 193–228, Yale University Press, New Haven & London, 1979.

Hsia, C.T., *The Classical Chinese Novel*, Columbia University Press, New York & London, 1968.

Hu Shih, 'The Establishment of Confucianism as a State Religion During the Han Dynasty', *Journal of the Royal Asiatic Society, North China Branch*, Vol. 60, 20–41. Shanghai, 1929.

Huang Pên-Ying, *I Ching Shên Hsüeh* (In Chinese), Hsin Feng, Hong Kong, n.d.

Ju-Lai Shên-Chang, Buddhist Palm, weekly martial arts comic strip periodical (in Chinese), Yu Lang Publishing, Hong Kong, 1982 onwards.

Jung, C.G., 'Synchronicity; an Acausal Connecting Principle', In *Collected Works*, Vol. 8, Routledge & Kegan Paul, London, 1960.

I Ching Chên Ch'uan, (Sung dynasty, in Chinese), Sao Yeh Shan Fang, no place of publication, 1869.

Kermadec, Jean-Michel Huon de, *Heavenly Pennies*, Unwin, Hemel Hempstead, 1985.

Knechtges, David R., *The Han Shu Biography of Yang Xiong*, Arizona State University, 1981.

Leban, Carl, Review of De Crespigny (1), *Journal of the American Oriental Society*, Vol 92, No 2, 344–345. April–June 1972.

Legge, James, *The Texts of Taoism*, 2 vols, (1891), Dover Books, New York, 1962.

——, *Confucius: Confucian Analects, The Great Learning, & The Doctrine of the Mean*, (1893), Dover Books, New York, 1971.

——, *The I Ching*, (1899), Dover Books, New York, 1963.

Lee, Jung Young, *The I Ching and Modern Man*, University Books Inc., New Jersey, 1975.

Li Han & Hsü Tzu-Kuang, *Meng Ch'iu; Famous Episodes from Chinese History and Legend*, Kodansha, Tokyo, 1979.

Li Shu Hua, *The South-pointing Carriage and the Mariner's Compass*, Yee Wen Publishing, Taiwan, 1959.

Lip, Evelyn, *Chinese Geomancy*, Times Books, Singapore, 1979.

Liu, Da, *The Tao and Chinese Culture*, Routledge & Kegan Paul, London, 1981.

Liu Ts'un-Yan, 'Taoist Self-Cultivation in Ming Thought', In William Theodore de Bary (ed), *Self and Society in Ming Thought*, 291–330, Columbia University Press, New York, 1970.

Liu Wu Chi, *A Short History of Confucian Philosophy*, Delta Books, New York, 1964.

Lo Kuan-Chung, *San Kuo Yen-i* (in Chinese), 2 vols, Chung Hua Shu Chu, Hong Kong, 1985.

Loewe, Michael, *Ways to Paradise*, George Allen & Unwin, London, 1979.

——, *Chinese Ideas of Life and Death*, George Allen & Unwin, London, 1982.

Loewe, Michael, & Blacker, Carmen (eds), *Divination and Oracles*, George Allen & Unwin, London, 1981.

Louton, John, 'Concepts of Comprehensiveness and Historical Change in the *Lü-Shih Ch'un-ch'iu*', In Henry Rosemont Jr (ed), *Explorations in Chinese Cosmology*, 105–118, JAAR Thematic Studies 50/2, Scholars Press, Chico, California, 1984.

Lu Hsun, *A Brief History of Chinese Fiction*, Foreign Languages Press, Peking, 1959.

Major, John S., 'The Five Phases, Magic Squares, and Schematic Cosmography', In Henry Rosemont Jr. (ed), *Explorations in Chinese Cosmology*, 133–166, JAAR Thematic Studies 50/2, Scholars Press, Chico, California, 1984.

Maspero, Henri, *Taoism and Chinese Religion*, University of

Massachusetts Press, Amherst, 1981.

Moore, Steve, 'Heaven's Reprimands', *Fortean Times*, No 41, 12–14, London, 1983.

Needham, Joseph, *Science and Civilisation in China*, Cambridge University Press, 1954 onwards.

Palmer, Martin, *T'ung Shu, The Ancient Chinese Almanac*, Rider, London, 1986.

Pang, Duane, 'The *P'u-Tu* Ritual', In Michael Saso and David W. Chappel (eds), *Buddhist and Taoist Studies 1*, University of Hawaii, 1977.

Po Hu T'ung, See Tjan.

Ritsema, Rudolf, 'The Great's Vigour', *Spring*, 1978, 183–206.

Romance of the Three Kingdoms: see Brewitt-Taylor.

San, J.H., *Ancient China's Inventions*, Commercial Press, Hong Kong, 1984.

San Kuo Chih: (In Chinese), 5 vols, Chung Hua Shu Chu, Peking, 1959.

Saso, Michael, *The Teachings of Taoist Master Chuang*, Yale University Press, New Haven, 1978.

——, 'What is the Ho T'u?', *History of Religions*, Vol 17, Nos 3 & 4, 399–416, Chicago, Feb–May, 1978.

Schafer, Edward H, *Pacing the Void*, University of California, 1977.

——, *Mirages on the Sea of Time*, University of California, 1985.

Shchutskii, Iulian K, *Researches on the I Ching*, Routledge & Kegan Paul, London, 1980.

Sherrill W.A., & Chu, W.K., *An Anthology of I Ching*, Routledge & Kegan Paul, London, 1977.

Shih Chi: see Watson (1), Yang & Yang.

Shu Ching: see Waltham/Legge.

Skinner, Stephen, *The Living Earth Manual of Feng Shui*, Routledge & Kegan Paul, London, 1982.

Soymie, M., 'China: The Struggle for Power', in *Larousse World Mythology*, 271–292, Paul Hamlyn, London, 1965.

Ssu-Ma Chien: see Watson (1), Yang & Yang.

Sung, Z.D., *The Text of Yi King*, (1935), Paragon Book Reprint Corp., New York, 1969.

Swanson, Gerald, *The Great Treatise*, Unpublished Ph.D. dissertation, University of Washington, 1974.

——, 'The Concept of Change in the Great Treatise' In Henry Rosemont Jr (ed), *Explorations in Chinese Cosmology*, 67–94, JAAR

Thematic Studies 50/2. Scholars Press, Chico, California, 1984.

Tan Manni, 'Chengdu: Cultural Shrines, Famous Food', *China Reconstructs*, Vol 29, No 10, 41, October 1980.

Tang Zhongpu, 'Storied Baidi Town', *China Reconstructs*, Vol 29, No 8, 49, August 1980.

Tjan Tjoe Som, *Po Hu T'ung; the Comprehensive Discussions in the White Tiger Hall*, 2 vols (consecutive page numbers), E.J. Brill, Leiden, 1949, 1952.

Waley, Arthur, 'The Book of Changes', offprint from *The Bulletin of the Museum of Far Eastern Antiquities*, No 5, 121–142, Stockholm, 1934.

Waltham/Legge, (James Legge translator, modernized by Clae Waltham), *Shu Ching*, George Allen & Unwin, London, 1972.

Ware, James R, *Alchemy, Medicine and Religion in the China of AD 320 (The Nei P'ien of Ko Hung)*, M.I.T. Press, Massachusetts, 1966.

Watson, Burton, *Records of the Grand Historian of China*, 2 vols, Columbia University Press, New York, 1961.

——, *Chuang Tzu, Basic Writings*, Columbia University Press, New York, 1964.

Wen Wu, (Cultural Relics), (in Chinese), Peking, 1974, No 7, No 9.

Werner, E.T.C., *Myths and Legends of China*, Harrap, London, 1922.

——, *A Dictionary of Chinese Mythology*, (1932), Julian Press, New York, 1961.

Whincup, Greg, *Rediscovering the I Ching*, Aquarian Press, Wellingborough, 1987.

Wilhelm, Hellmut, *Change*, Routledge & Kegan Paul, London, 1961.

——, *Heaven, Earth and Man in the Book of Changes*, University of Washington Press, Seattle, 1977.

Wilhelm/Baynes (Translated by Richard Wilhelm, English by Cary F. Baynes), *I Ching, or Book of Changes*, Routledge & Kegan Paul, London, 1968.

Williams, C.A.S., *Outlines of Chinese Symbolism and Art Motives*, (1941), Charles E Tuttle, Vermont & Tokyo, 1974.

De Woskin, Kenneth J., *Doctors, Diviners, and Magicians of Ancient China: Biographies of Fang-shih*, Columbia University Press, New York, 1983.

Wu, Liu Ch'iang, & Davis, Tenney, L., 'An Ancient Chinese Treatise on Alchemy Entitled Ts'an T'ung Ch'i', *Isis*, No 53, (Vol 18, pt 2), 210–289, St. Catherine Press, Bruges, 1932.

Yang, Hsien-yi, & Yang, Gladys, *Records of the Historian*, Commercial Press, Hong Kong, 1974.

Yao Chên Tsung, *San Kuo I Wên Chih* (*Bibliography of the Three Kingdoms*), (In Chinese, late 19th century). Excerpted in *Chu-ko Liang Chi* (q.v.), xxv–xxx.

Xiong Gou Zhen, 'Researches on Philosophy', *Beijing Review*, Vol 24, No 2, 31, Beijing, 12 January 1981.

Index